ALL THINGS NEW

*The Story of the
Sisters of St. Joseph
of Carondelet
in the
Los Angeles Province*

By Mary Williams CSJ

Good Ground Press
Sisters of St. Joseph of Carondelet
1884 Randolph Avenue, St. Paul, MN 55105

Pictured on the front cover are sisters of St. Joseph in traditional CSJ ministries of healthcare, teaching, working with the deaf, and direct service to the poor—Sr. Adele O'Sullivan MD, Sr. Thomas Mary Collins in her lifelong ministry to the deaf, and Sisters Marilyn Rudy and Louise Bernstein, founders of St. Joseph Center.

In describing the sisters' ministry to the Native Americans in the early chapters, I have used the familiar tribal names which were used at that time. Since then, the Papagos have largely rejected that name, returning to the original Tohono O'odham. The Yumas are now known as the Quechan Tribe.

For copies of *All Things New* contact:
Sisters of St. Joseph of Carondelet
11999 Chalon Road
Los Angeles, CA 90049
Phone: 310-889-2138 or email iatye@csjla.org

Cover design: Carol L. Smith, CSJ

ISBN: 978-1-885996-00-8

Credit: Vicky McCargar's article "From the Archives", included in Chapter 6, was published in the Summer/Fall 2011 issue of *The Mount*. Used with permission of Mount St. Mary's College.

Copyright ©2014 Mary Williams. All rights reserved. Printed in the U.S.A. Material in this book may not be reproduced in whole or in part in any form or format without special permission from the publisher.

*To the
Sisters of St. Joseph—
the pioneers who founded
and developed the Los Angeles
Province, and those of us who
are also pioneers carrying our
mission into a future of all
things new.*

TABLE OF CONTENTS

FOREWORD	7
CHAPTERS	
1. Crossing the desert	9
2. Expanding on the frontier	18
3. Serving on the Indian missions	30
4. California foundations	44
5. Pioneers in the Northwest	60
6. Building the Mount	75
7. Post-war explosion of growth	91
8. Stirrings of change with Vatican II	105
9. Serving a changing culture	119
10. New ways of announcing the Good News	132
11. Listening to the cry of the poor	147
12. Behold, I am making something new	161
AFTERWORD	173
A NEW HARVEST	175
PROVINCIAL LEADERSHIP, LOS ANGELES PROVINCE	176
NOTES	178
WORKS CITED	183
ABOUT THE AUTHOR	187

FOREWORD

All Things New was written during a time of congregation-wide conversation and discernment as the Sisters of St. Joseph of Carondelet prepared for the July 2013 Congregational Chapter. The world was changing, seeming to shift on its axis. Our lives as women religious had been changing for a long time, and we were coming to terms with what it all meant. We knew one thing for sure—we were moving into an unknown future. The Chapter's theme from Isaiah—*I am making something new! Do you not see it?* (43:19)—spoke powerfully to all of us as we looked ahead.

I finished the last chapter of this book in June 2013, a month before Chapter began in Los Angeles. As I thought about the Chapter theme and the story of our journey in the west, I began to see that the experience of **new** runs as a theme through all our history. I thought of the Irish sister of St. Joseph tending to a dying woman in a dark tent in the Arizona desert, and of the sister in the black habit walking the darkness of an inner-city Los Angeles night looking for abandoned women to bring home to a shelter. We weren't brought up for this, and our education did not prepare us for it. Frequently we didn't know the language or the culture. We had not been taught how to start hospitals, how to buy real estate and found a college, or how to bring together imprisoned women with their children. All through our history it has been a journey of faith, sometimes blind faith, to find and minister to the neighbor.

All Things New has been a wonderful story to tell and a profound experience for all of us who worked on this CSJ history. There are many people to thank. I am grateful to our leadership team who gave me encouragement and resources to do the travel, research and writing. Bishop Carlos Sevilla's advice gave me the jump-start I needed to begin the project, and he was a source of encouragement throughout. He had the patience to read the manuscript when it was close to completion. My brother Hill Williams read the book as it developed, chapter by chapter, helping me to bring it to a broader audience. Sr. Karen Kennelly read it from the viewpoint of a published historian. Sr. Sandra Williams's reading gave me special help in interpretation of our post-Vatican II years. Other CSJs contributed to putting the story together, helping with interviews, running down elusive dates, and sharing treasured memories. The province staff, particularly Sr. Mary Agnes Nance, Sr. Carol Smith, and Sr. Irma Amelia Tye, have put their time and expertise behind the task of getting the book into the hands of readers. Many others supported me with their encouragement—my sister, my family and friends, so many CSJs, particularly the sisters at Carondelet Center who watched me come and go in my visits to the Los Angeles archives and cheered me on.

Special thanks go to the small committee who shared the project with me. Sr. Thomas Bernard MacConnell, Sr. Mary Murphy, and Sr. Patricia Rose Shanahan each brought her special passions and skills. Chapter by chapter, we huddled around the little round table in the archives office, arguing over details and wording, putting things in and taking things out. I am deeply grateful for their steady help and encouragement.

Gifted CSJ historians preceded me on this path. At times, I felt as if I were walking with friends as I read their journals and letters, scholarly works and articles. Sr. Monica Corrigan's journal of the original trek was a treasured resource. Letters home and journals of the early sisters, especially Sr. Mary John Berchmans Hartrich and Mother Julia Littenecker, brought the story alive. Some wrote with a sharp sense of history like Sr. Mary Dolorosa Mannix, Sr. Alberta Cammack, Sr. Aloysia Ames, Sr. Mary Jean Fields, and Sr. Mary Ellen Sprouffske. The published histories of the Sisters of St. Joseph by Sr. Lucida Savage (1927) and Sister St. Claire Coyne (1966) have been invaluable monuments of our story.

My thanks go to the generous assistance of the archivists who are preserving the history of the congregation: Sr. Rita Louise Huebner, congregational archivist; Sr. Jane Behlmann, St. Louis archivist; and Victoria McCargar, Mount St. Mary's College archivist who unearthed the tantalizing two stories about the Mount's purchase of the Chalon property. Sr. Patricia Rose Shanahan, Los Angeles Province archivist, has been a valued collaborator throughout the writing of the book. Without the rich and beautifully organized archives in our province, this book would not have happened.

CHAPTER 1

CROSSING THE DESERT

"The city was illuminated—fireworks in full play. Balls of combustible matter were thrown in the streets through which we passed; at each explosion Sister Euphrasia made the sign of the Cross."

— Monica Corrigan CSJ

    The history of the Sisters of St. Joseph of Carondelet in the Los Angeles Province began with fireworks, pealing bells, and a community celebration in the small frontier town of Tucson, Arizona. It was about 6 p.m. on May 26, 1870—Ascension Thursday.

    Seven tired, dusty, and travel-worn sisters were arriving after thirty-six days of exhausting and dangerous travel from their motherhouse in Carondelet, Missouri. They had traveled by rail from St. Louis to San Francisco on the newly completed transcontinental railroad, by ocean steamer to San Diego, and on a wagon trail for the final trek to Tucson. On that lonely and sometimes frightening trek across the desert, frequently accompanied only by their driver, they probably weren't prepared for the boisterous western greeting in the little desert town.

    The story actually began 34 years before when six Sisters of St. Joseph arrived in New Orleans from Lyons, France, in 1836, and made the trip up the Mississippi River to St. Louis at the invitation of Bishop Joseph Rosati. The little group settled in Carondelet, a village near St. Louis, and set to work teaching and responding to the needs they saw around them. The spread of the community was rapid, following the Mississippi River up to Minnesota and the Ohio River into the Northeast.

Pressing need was everywhere as the nation expanded in the years after the Civil War. Soon Reverend Mother St. John Facemaz heard from Bishop John Baptist Lamy, bishop of Santa Fe, who wrote in 1868 asking her to send sisters to Tucson, "being the capital of Arizona with a population of about three thousand people, more than half of them Catholics, and the others will be disposed for the establishment of our school there....There is a great deal of good to be done there."[1]

By the following year, Tucson had its own bishop, John Baptist Salpointe, who thanked Reverend Mother for promising some sisters for the Tucson mission. Preparations in Tucson were well underway. "I can tell you that the house will not need too much change for commencing a school. It has three large rooms for school rooms, a work room for the Sisters, a parlor, a large sleeping room, a refectory, kitchen and storeroom. All these on the ground floor, in two rows separated by a long covered corridor which, in warm weather, can serve as a recreation room for the little girls." There was still work to do, though. "As to furnishings, there are none for the moment, but we will have some."[2]

The seven sisters who arrived in Tucson in 1870. Seated from left Sisters Ambrosia Arnichaud, Martha Peters, Maximus Croissat. Standing from left Sisters Emerentia Bonnefoy, Euphrasia Suchet, Monica Corrigan, Hyacinth Blanc

Mother St. John had to wait until after the novices made their profession of vows in March 1870 before she could make final plans for the group she would send to Tucson. Five of the volunteers were French, having come to Carondelet as professed sisters from Moutiers: Mother Emerentia Bonnefoy, superior, and Sisters Ambrosia Arnichaud, Euphrasia Suchet, Hyacinth Blanc, and Maximus Croissat. The other two had entered the community at Carondelet: Sisters Monica Corrigan, a native of Canada, and Martha Peters, an Irish lay sister. They were all young, ranging in age from 27 to 37.

It was fortunate that Mother St. John delayed the missionaries' departure until 1870. The transcontinental railroad had been completed just the year before, linking the existing railroads of the eastern United States with the Pacific coast. It stretched from Omaha, Nebraska, which had been the western terminus of the Union Pacific Railroad, to Oakland, California, across the bay from San Francisco. If the sisters had traveled earlier, the trip overland by stagecoach

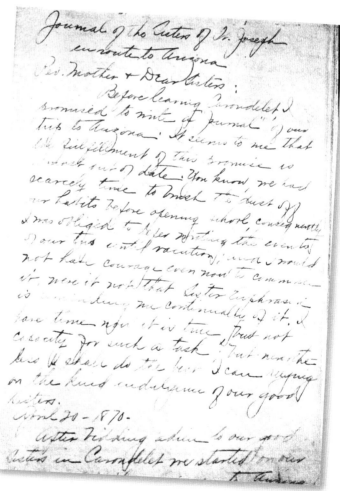

Sr. Monica Corrigan's diary – beginning

would have been more hazardous and much longer. The railroad trip took the sisters five days and was safer and cheaper, an economy fare costing about $65.

But along with the excitement of new landscapes and interesting people, the journey was not without its dangers and inconveniences. Sr. Monica Corrigan told the story of the "long and perilous journey" of the seven sisters in her journal,a treasured document in the

Monica Corrigan was a widow and a convert to Catholicism when she became a Sister of St. Joseph. Born Annie Taggert in the province of Quebec in 1843, she became a university teacher of mathematics and married John Corrigan. They settled in Kansas City and had two children before an epidemic of black diphtheria left her childless and a widow within a few days.

St. Teresa's Academy in Kansas City needing a math teacher, Annie went to live and teach at the Academy, and was soon attracted to the Catholic faith and to religious life. She entered the novitiate of the Sisters of St. Joseph at Carondelet in St. Louis receiving the habit and her name—Sister Monica of the Sacred Heart—on December 8, 1869.

All accounts of Monica describe her as courageous, fearless, independent, compassionate, and sometimes a maverick. She gave invaluable service to the new St. Joseph community in Tucson in many ways, raising funds, negotiating contracts and agreements with the city, counties, railroads, and mining companies. She traveled in Mexico and Arizona soliciting support for the new academy building from ranchers and miners, and looking at the possibility of opening schools in Mexico. Sr. Monica was probably equal to the best businessmen in her financial and business skills, and assertive enough in one of her positions that the local bishop asked her superiors to move her to California!

One of her greatest services was to begin the monumental task of research for the first history of the Congregation—hand-copying early correspondence and writing to sisters throughout the Congregation asking them for their recollections of early foundations.

But perhaps her most memorable adventure was as one of the original seven sisters who made the trek across half the nation by railroad, ship, and covered wagon to establish the first foundation in the West in 1870. Her gift for observation and writing, her sense of humor, and her zest for life brought that story alive in her treasured diary of the journey of the Sisters of St. Joseph to Arizona. [3]

history of the sisters coming to the West. She tells how they started out from St. Louis on April 20, visiting two convents there in town to say goodbye and taking the train to Kansas City for more farewells, perhaps wondering if they would ever see their friends again. Then, accompanied by Mother St. John for a last goodbye, they continued on to Omaha to make connections with the San Francisco train.

From April 23 until April 27, they traveled across the great American plains, crossed the Rockies, passed along the shores of Salt Lake, and crossed more mountains as they came into Nevada and California. All this while, they got little sleep or privacy, sitting up at night, until some kind friends were able to get them two sleeping berths for the last few nights. "When we retired at night, the heat was as oppressive as that of a St. Louis July; the mornings were as cold as a Canadian March." [4]

Reaching San Francisco at 7 p.m. on April 27, they were received cordially at the hospital of the Sisters of Mercy. "We presented a beautiful sight after our week's journey without arranging our toilet. We were sadly in need of rest, as we were completely dizzy from the motion of the cars." After a few days with the Sisters of Mercy, their journey continued on the ocean steamer "Orizaba" arriving in San Diego on Tuesday morning, May 3.

Bishop Salpointe had planned to meet the missionaries in San Diego and accompany them on the last part of the trip, but Reverend Mother's letter failed to reach him in time, so the sisters made their own arrangements, engaged a covered wagon and driver, and set off on a wagon trail for Arizona May 7. The wagon was too small to allow all seven sisters to ride inside, so one rode outside with the driver.

"About 10 o'clock we passed a white post that marks the southwest boundary of the United States. We dropped a few tears at the sight of it, then entered Lower California." At the end of the day, they camped at the foot of a mountain, made some tea, and took their supper off a rock. Sleep was hard those cold nights. The first night three sisters slept under the wagon, two lay inside, and Sisters Euphrasia and Monica sat up in a corner of the wagon trying to sleep. When Sr. Euphrasia woke screaming one night with one of the horses licking her face, the others were sure she had been attacked by wolves.

As they pushed farther east, they experienced courteous protection by their driver, kind acts of hospitality along the way, and great curiosity and interest in this wagon-full of women religious. On the second day, some ranchers earnestly proposed marriage to them, "saying we would do better by accepting the offer than by going to Tucson, for we would be all massacred by the Indians. The simplicity and earnestness with which they spoke put indignation out of the question, as it was evident that they meant no insult, but our good." At another stop, they encountered a rowdy group of men, some drunk, who annoyed and frightened them, coming in and out of the shanty where they were trying to sleep. "We asked the cook what it all meant; he replied in a somewhat embarrassed manner that ladies seldom passed this way and when they do, the men wish to enjoy their society."

On the third day, the group reached the mountains at the entrance of the American Desert. "We were obliged to travel it on foot; at the highest point it is said to be 4,000 feet above sea level. We were compelled to stop here to breathe. Some of the Sisters lay down on the road side, being unable to proceed farther. Besides this terrible fatigue, we suffered still more from thirst." Coming down those boulder-strewn mountains, they saw teams of horses, oxen and cattle that had died trying to ascend. "At one place we counted fourteen oxen which had apparently died at the same time." Sr. Maximus called it the "Abomination of Desolation."

On May 10, they entered the desert. "It is a vast bed of sand; traveling over it is rendered dangerous, on account of the sand storms….As sand is a good conductor, consequently the heat is extreme. When the sun is at meridian height, the sand is hot enough to blister." For the next few days, the little group traveled by night as much as they could, to avoid the intense desert heat. They were told of a stagecoach with seven passengers found buried in the sand. "In one place, we passed a drove of horned cattle said to contain 1,000 head; every one died of heat the same day. Another place we passed the remains of 1,500 sheep, smothered in a sand storm." They frequently walked beside the wagon to keep the wheels from sinking into the deep sand. "We could get water only in one place, and when we did get it, it was not only hot but so full of minerals that we suffered more after taking it than before."

On May 11, they came to a ranch where they were met with great kindness. "We were at once accommodated with water to wash, a refreshment we sorely needed as we had not washed since we left San Diego. You may imagine our condition after our weary trip. One of the Sisters wore low shoes; her feet and ankles were very painful, and it was with difficulty that she removed her stockings, as they stuck to the flesh with the blood which had congealed there. After getting them off, she found 22 bleeding sores, produced by the cactus plant with which the desert abounds."

Resting by day and traveling much of the night, they entered Arizona Territory, carved from New Mexico Territory only a few years earlier. After a near disastrous ferry crossing of the Colorado River, they reached Fort Yuma and were greeted by Father Francisco Jouvenceau, Vicar General of Tucson, who had been sent by Bishop Salpointe to accompany the sisters the rest of the way to Tucson. After a few days rest, they set off again, this time in comparative comfort, "having a comfortable covered carriage, good Father Francisco to guard us, a plentiful supply of provisions, etc., and a cook to prepare our meals. We had a tent to sleep under but as it was rather small, some of us slept in the wagon on the seats."

In the last phase of the trek, they encountered a peaceful group of Pima Indians. Stopping at noon, they found a place to rest in the ruins of some old buildings. "Mother went there to rest and fell asleep. A troop of nude Indians came in the meantime, who were peaceable; they had the consideration to be quiet, and let her sleep. Sister Martha was resting on an old cowhide; a noble warrior perceiving her, stole softly up and sat down beside her as her Guardian Angel."

But, unknown to the travelers, the most perilous part of the trek was

Picacho Peak

immediately ahead. That evening, sixteen soldiers rode up to the encampment and said they had been sent to escort some travelers. "The Indians are afraid to appear when they hear the soldiers, unless they are sufficiently strong in number to fight them," Sr. Monica wrote. These were the Apaches, at their most fierce during this time because of their anger over government efforts to herd them into reservations, a result of the ironically named Indian Peace Policy. Attacks on travelers were frequent and deadly, particularly at Picacho Peak, a mountain pass outside of Tucson. "A fearful massacre had been perpetrated there only a week previous. The road winds through the narrow pass in the mountains, where the Indians conceal themselves and throw out their poisoned arrows…The place is literally filled with graves—sorrowful monuments of savage barbarity."

By now, the sisters had not only the soldiers to protect them. They began to be joined by citizens of Tucson who had ridden out to escort the travelers. Three miners also joined the group for protection. Around midnight, "each one prepared his fire-arms; even good Father Francisco. The citizens pressed around our carriage. The soldiers rode about like bloodhounds in search of prey. In passing through the peak, the horses began to neigh which is a sure indication of the close proximity of the savages. 'The Indians! The Indians!' was echoed from every mouth. Whip and spurs were given to the horses—we went like lightning—the men yelling all the while like so many fiends, in order to frighten the savages. The novelty of the scene kept us from being afraid. We traveled in this manner until four o'clock a.m." [5]

The arrival of the Sisters of St. Joseph into Tucson on May 26 was told by Bishop Salpointe in a letter to Mother St. John, dated June 3, 1870. "It was the beautiful day of the Ascension at nightfall when the pious colony made its entrance into our capital. The good Sisters in their humility had chosen this advanced hour, thinking thus they would not attract any attention and demonstrations of joy and recognition which the people had prepared for them. As to the celebration, nothing was lost; everyone was in the street of the town, Protestants and Catholics alike, to give welcome and feteing to those sent by Providence. I leave to the Sisters the task of telling you in detail of the fireworks displayed in their honor and to inform you of the discharging of firearms that was heard in all parts of the city, which continued to an advanced hour of the night." [6]

The townsfolk escorted the sisters to their home that had been lovingly prepared for them. The bishop was waiting there to welcome them, along with several men and women who brought them water so they could wash and then served them a warm meal. When the visitors were gone, the sisters were left in quiet possession of their new home.

The long trek from St. Louis was over at last and they were at home in their little adobe house, but they did not take much time to rest. According to Sr. Monica, they barely had time to brush the dust of the trail off their habits when school opened on June 6, 1870—eleven days after they arrived. The ministry of the Sisters of St. Joseph in the West had begun.

Sr. Monica Corrigan's diary – ending

Chapter 2

Expanding on the frontier

"The day these pious and devoted ladies came to Tucson was considered with reason, by all the friends of education and civilization, as the opening of a new era for Arizona."

—Bishop John Baptist Salpointe

Those first few weeks and months, despite the excitement and zeal of the sisters, must have demanded a great deal of courage. Their surroundings could not have been more new to them. Their home was a one-story building with thick adobe walls and a roof of sagebrush and cactus interlaced on pine rafters and covered with mud. Sr. John Berchmans Hartrich, who arrived in Tucson six years later, referred in her diary to the "mud houses" in which they lived and continued, "the floors are not of boards; very few have them….some put a thin layer of coarse sand to prevent mud when the floors are watered, which is done once or twice a day to make it cool and keep down the dust which is very plentiful here."

Tucson in the early 1870s was on a rough and dangerous frontier. A German immigrant who arrived there in 1872 described his first impressions of the little town. "The streets were untidy and the houses were one-story adobe with dirt roofs and dirt floors. The furniture was mostly handmade. Cooking stoves were scarce, and cooking was done in chimneys or outside in Dutch ovens. There were no sidewalks, no trees, nor vegetation of any kind….There was no telegraph nor telephone. For light there were coal oil lamps in some stores and saloons, but oil was very expensive. The Apaches were a constant threat to the peace and safety of the people." [1]

Mount St. Joseph, first provincial house, Tucson. From left Sisters Ildephonse, St. Peter, Guadalupe, Gabriel. On the left is Sr. Guadalupe's sister.

Sister John Berchmans just exclaimed, "In all my days I never saw such a barren, sandy, deserted place, as out here."

When the Congregation of St. Joseph was founded in the mid-1600s, the first sisters were told to go out and divide the city, and to meet the needs of the people where they found them. In no way did Tucson qualify as a city, but the charism of the sisters held true. On this American frontier, they began to reach out to those who needed them. And they started with education.

Their first school began in the simple adobe structure the bishop had prepared for them, a combination of convent and school. It became the future St. Joseph's Academy, the first school in Arizona for American children. But it was originally called "the French school" by the townspeople because most of the sisters were French. Enrollment quickly grew, including both Catholic and non-Catholic children, mostly from Spanish and Mexican families. Since the majority of the children understood only Spanish, the sisters added another task to their full days, diligently studying Spanish in their free time.

In the first years of the school, no provision could be made for children unable to pay tuition, so the sisters set aside one classroom in the overcrowded school for the poor and offered religion classes every Sunday in both English and Spanish for children who could not enroll in the school. A letter to the County Superintendent of Schools in December 1875 gives a glimpse of the circumstances in that little classroom. "Since you are so kind as to allow us the privilege of making suggestions to promote the school interest, we respectfully beg leave to call your attention…to St. Joseph's Parochial School. This school was established for and is patronized by the *poor*….The children attending it are so poor that half of them, at least, are actually losing their time for want of books etc. We have provided a teacher (a Sister) and a room as well furnished as we could afford, but it is absolutely impossible for us, under present circumstances, to supply the children with all the books etc. they need." [2]

Within a few years, new appeals extended the sisters' ministry into the Indian missions. In 1873, Bishop Salpointe asked them to open a school for the Papago Indians at San Xavier del Bac Mission about nine miles south of Tucson. The mission which had flourished under the Jesuits and Franciscans had been abandoned with the overthrow of Spain's colonial government in Mexico in 1822. Now that the Papago tribe had come under the protection of the United States government, Bishop Salpointe saw the opportunity of opening a school there and turned once again to the Sisters of St. Joseph.

Sisters Euphrasia and Maximus left the other sisters behind in the Tucson school and set off down the old mission road, arriving at San Xavier to find the buildings in ruins. But six rooms at the mission were soon made usable for classrooms, and the school began to flourish. Unfortunately, the Department of the Interior ordered the Papago and the Pima agencies to be consolidated three years later, and the school had to be closed. The sisters would not be returning to San Xavier to restore the school until 1888.

Meanwhile, at the request of Bishop Salpointe, more sisters were sent from Carondelet to add numbers to the little Tucson group. Sisters Lucretia Burns, Francesca Kelly, and Mary Martha Dunne left Kansas City on December 1, 1873, accompanied by Bishop Salpointe. Their story was told later to Sr. Monica Corrigan who always had an eye for history. The sisters traveled by rail until they reached Kit

Carson, Colorado, and then left for Tucson by wagon on December 13. Late on the first day out, they lost their way in a snowstorm and arrived at a sheep ranch. The two shepherds let them spend the night in their little house, while they cooked and slept out on the hillside, never speaking a word to the women. The sisters rested in the room, and the bishop wrapped himself in blankets and lay across the door.

The next night, still lost, they slept in a deserted cabin. "Sr. Mary wrapped the two sisters up bambino style and with a log for a pillow they rested." A sudden noise in the night alarmed them all, but "the sisters were tied up so tight they could not get up." Proceeding in short stages, they finally arrived in Tucson on January 27, 1874.[3]

Their arrival brought the number of the Arizona missionaries to ten, and Sr. Francesca Kelly soon joined the San Xavier sisters. But within that same year, Sr. Emerentia, superior of the little group, died. A native of Moutiers, France, she had come to Carondelet in 1859, had served as superior of the community in Oswego, New York, and then had volunteered as missionary to Arizona. The fatigue of the journey west, the change of climate, and the many privations of a new mission took a toll on her naturally delicate health, and she died on August 1, 1874, the first of the missionaries to die.

A third group of sisters arrived in Tucson in June 1876. Sisters Basil Morris, Mary Rose Dorna, Eutichiana Piccini, and Mary John Berchmans Hartrich began their trip by train to San Francisco. They continued by steamer around Baja California, eventually transferring to a smaller boat to travel up the Colorado River to Fort Yuma. After ten more days of travel on lonely desert roads, they covered the last 300 miles of their trip, and arrived in Tucson on June 7. Sr. John Berchmans kept a lively diary, filled with detailed observations and high humor. After a description of the mud and cactus roofs of the houses, she comments, "If you wish to have a better idea, just look at a hay loft." But later she calls the adobe houses beautiful because "you have no idea how cool these houses are." She appreciated the Mexican people, always finding "the people on our way very kind and obliging, much more so than in the states. The people generally are very poor, but still are as happy as if they owned great possessions."

Aware of the difficulties of communication and transportation

Sr. Mary Joseph Franco

Born in Tucson in 1862, eight-year-old Virginia Franco would have been among the three thousand townspeople who used fireworks to celebrate the arrival of the first seven Sisters of St. Joseph to her home city in 1870. The French-speaking sisters quickly learned Spanish in order to speak with Virginia and her friends. In 1877, Virginia came to Mount St. Joseph to enter the novitiate. Given the name Sr. Mary Joseph, she made her first vows in 1880. For the pioneer sisters, the Southwest with its saguaro and cactus was foreign territory; to Sr. Mary Joseph, it was home.

Sr. Mary Joseph had her first mission experience at St. Mary's Hospital across the dusty road from Mount St. Joseph. In 1886, she became one of the founders of the Indian school at Fort Yuma. In 1889, she helped open St. Mary's Academy in Los Angeles, but soon returned to her beloved Yuma Indians and stayed there until the sisters withdrew in 1900.

These early assignments prepared Sr. Mary Joseph for her mission of missions, St. John's, Komatke. For 29 years, she would be partner to the deprivation and love, destitution and hope known as Komatke. Her good friend, Sr. Alphonse Lamb, once described her as full of fun. She took this quality to Komatke, a physically harsh and desolate mission. She also brought her remarkable skills in needlework, her great love of music, and her talent for learning languages.

Upon arriving at St. John's, she learned the Pima language. Then she began to learn Maricopa from one of their students, explaining, "It is so much like Yuma." Eventually eight tribes were represented at the school, including the Apaches. Geronimo, the great Apache chief, would have been happy to know that his grandson was a student at Komatke.

Staying at Komatke until 1930, Sr. Mary Joseph went to St. Boniface Indian School in Banning for a rest, hoping to have her health restored. She died there, far from her many loves and cares. But her legacy lives on. She died one year before the birth of her grand niece Sr. Mary Elena Lopez CSJ who was named Virginia for this treasured grand aunt. And the legacy continues on with another niece Anita Franco Chichotka, the daughter of Ralph Franco, Sr. Mary Joseph's youngest brother. Both Anita and her daughter Michele Swallow are CSJ Associates in Los Angeles.

Mary Murphy, CSJ [4]

between Carondelet and Arizona, and with the encouragement of Bishop Salpointe, Reverend Mother St. John Facemaz had begun planning for a western province as early as the sisters' first year in Tucson. On May 7, 1876, final permission was given by the Holy See, and the Arizona Province was established. Mother Irene Facemaz was appointed provincial, Mother Louis Alexis Dunand became novice mistress, and the search began for a province center.
A property was selected in the foothills west of town and construction begun on a small adobe house to house the provincialate and novitiate. The simple building, named Mount St. Joseph, was the home of the first novices—Sisters Teresa Ortiz, Mary Agnes Orosco, Mary Amelia Leon, Clara Otero, Mary Joseph Franco, and Mary John Noli.

Mother Irene remained in Tucson for only one year, and was succeeded by Mother Mary Basil Morris who received in 1878 a request to open a hospital in the north part of Arizona Territory. The request came from the Santa Fe Railroad which saw the need for a hospital in Prescott, at that time the territorial capital of Arizona, for employees and miners. Sisters John Berchmans Hartrich, Mary Martha Dunne and Mary Rose Doran set out on the week's journey by stage to Prescott. They opened their hospital on September 6, 1878 in a small frame house divided into two sections—the sisters' living quarters on one side, and sick and accident victims on the other. Primitive equipment and furnishings were financed by the sisters' begging, supplemented with funds furnished by John C. Fremont, military governor of Arizona territory, and his wife, Jessie Benton Fremont. Patients in the small hospital paid their bills in eggs, potatoes, and occasionally a few dollars. The sisters also held classes for the Catholic children of the town in the frame house during times when patients were few.

In 1880, at the request of the Southern Pacific Railroad, Bishop Salpointe opened a 12-bed hospital in Tucson on a 60-acre tract of land across the road from Mount St. Joseph. Once more, he turned to the Sisters of St. Joseph, this time to staff his little hospital. The sisters were not new to health care, having become accustomed to caring for the poor and the sick in Tucson. Mother Basil became administrator of the hospital, assisted by three sisters who not only cared for the patients, but did all the manual labor as well, washing

Cornerstone for St. Mary's Hospital, 1880

and ironing all the linens, scrubbing floors and preparing food.

In 1881, Mother Gonzaga Grand succeeded Mother Basil as provincial superior, remaining in office until 1890. At the time of her appointment, the General Chapter minutes of June 6th describe the newest province in the congregation: "The Vicariate Apostolic of Arizona numbers five houses which by the authority of the Holy See have been erected into a separate province. Among the houses of the Province of Arizona are one academy, three select and three parochial schools and two hospitals. The number of professed sisters is 25 who are employed in teaching 490 pupils and about 59 patients. The number of patients received last year is 650."[5]

Calm and deeply spiritual, Mother Gonzaga came with years of experience in community leadership and in business dealings, directing the province through a decade of active expansion. Seeing the opportunity of improving conditions at Bishop Salpointe's hospital, she negotiated with the diocese in 1882 to purchase the hospital and grounds for $20,000. This was the seed of Tucson's St. Mary's Hospital which has served southern Arizona for well over 100 years.

In 1883, four sisters arrived in Florence, 85 miles north of Tucson, to staff the parish school. Most of the people in Florence were farmers who paid their children's tuition with vegetables and honey. One of the parents brought the sisters fresh milk every morning. "The sisters got their water from a barrel kept by a canal near their

St. Mary's, first hospital in Arizona. On the left, the sisters' convent with the hospital in the center. The sanatorium for tubercular patients, completed in 1900, on the right.

St. Mary's sanatorium

grounds. Their lifestyle included shaking out clothing and shoes each morning to dislodge scorpions and centipedes, a precaution to be taken before dressing and hurrying to morning prayers." [6] Florence had shown promise of growth because of its proximity to silver mines, but hopes faded when railroads bypassed the little town. After the sisters had ministered in Florence for six years, the town could no longer support the school and the sisters had to withdraw.

But memories of the sisters remained. During the six years in Florence, Sr. Angeline Fitzpatrick, twenty-three years old and much

The sisters' school at Florence

loved in the town, had died. When the sisters left Florence, the people would not let them disinter her body. If they could not keep the living sisters of St. Joseph, at least they would keep their dear Sr. Angeline. "Some time after the sisters' departure children reported seeing a sister in the field near the old convent. The pastor and some people hurried to the convent but found it in its usual abandoned condition. It then began to be rumored that the children had seen an apparition of Sr. Angeline. Similar apparitions were reported, but the rumors ceased after the priest celebrated Mass for the repose of Sr. Angeline's soul." [7]

In 1885, Mother Gonzaga was able to purchase property near the new St. Augustine cathedral to build a new and enlarged St. Joseph's Academy. But money was scarce, the bishop was unable to help financially, so the sisters got permission to beg help from the miners in Arizona and Sonora. Sr. Monica Corrigan was in charge of the begging project which was so successful that the new two-story stone building was completed a year later. When St. Joseph's Academy moved to its new home in 1886, the sisters were able to convert the former adobe building into a parochial school for the poor children of the town. Mother Gonzaga moved the provincialate and novitiate to the new St. Joseph's Academy the same year. At the request of

Bishop Peter Bourgade, the new bishop of Tucson, the small adobe house that had been the first home of the western province became St. Joseph's Orphan Home.

Since the sisters received no financial help for the orphan home, they supported it by begging, making regular visits to merchants and residents of Tucson asking for food, clothing, and fuel for the children. Salpointe wrote of St. Joseph's home: "The place is a very appropriate one, out of the town and very healthy with extensive playgrounds and gardens, and what astonishes the visitors is that no state aid whatever is furnished to the sisters to extend the benefit of their kind attention to a greater number of poor destitute children."[8] To Sr. St. Peter Ryan, the first supervisor of the home, it made no difference "whether the children who came to the Home were white, black or yellow. Once they were there, they were her treasures and joy."[9]

St. Joseph's Academy, second location of the Arizona provincialate and novitiate, 1886

The home flourished until 1901 when a cyclone struck Tucson, tearing off the roof of the home and damaging it beyond repair. At this tragic loss, Sr. Angelica Byrne took the initiative, setting about obtaining land and money to finance the rebuilding. A benefactor gave her a deed to forty acres of land several miles south of Tucson, specifying the gift not for the diocese nor for the Sisters of St. Joseph, but rather for the orphan children of Arizona. Then Sr. Angelica began to travel to mining camps, frequently being lowered by basket into the mines, appealing to the miners for funds to care for the orphan children. It took four years, traveling by foot, by stage, and sometimes in the caboose of freight trains to the mining camps. Although she had a pass from the railroad allowing her to ride in the caboose on her begging journeys, not everyone was so understanding. Once, returning home to Tucson from the mines, she was challenged by a conductor several miles east of home. Refusing even to look at her pass, he stopped the train and put sister and her young companion out in the desert. It was a long lonely walk home that day. But at the end, she had forty acres of land and $16,000, and the new orphan home could be built, a two-story building in a grove of peppers and oleanders, able to house one hundred children.

Another school was opened the next year in Prescott. In the years since the sisters had opened their hospital there in 1878, they had purchased the hospital building and property, improved it, and continued to operate it, but the need for a hospital in the town had decreased steadily. In 1886, Bishop Bourgade visited Prescott and recognized the need for a school. He wrote to Mother Julia Litteneker, assistant general and director of missions, on July 13, 1886: "I can see no hope for the hospital. On the other hand, from what I can see and hear, the hopes for a school are very good, even for a boarding school. No risks to be run as you have the building and most of the furniture, much good to be done. You are not going to keep four sisters here for a sick man to come occasionally....Let us get on without delay. Bear this in mind, Mother, the best opportunities are often lost here in this country by inopportune delay. I am decidedly in favor of the school."[10]

Acting quickly on the bishop's advice, the sisters remodeled the hospital building and opened Prescott's St. Joseph's Academy in the fall term of 1886 with a healthy enrollment. A boarding and day school, St. Joseph's prospered, quickly outgrowing its first space. With a generous gift of ten acres on a height overlooking the city and mountainous surroundings, the new St. Joseph's Academy was built in 1904, under the direction of Mother Aurelia Mary Doyle. The academy, the pioneer Catholic school in northern Arizona, continued to serve the education needs of northern Arizona for many years. [11]

Despite the rapid expansion of the ministry of the Sisters of St. Joseph in the Southwest and the completion of railroad connections from St. Louis to Tucson in March, 1880, the new province did not flourish in the early years. Unlike St. Louis and other eastern provinces, faraway Arizona in the late 1800s did not attract young women wishing to become sisters. Only six women, all Arizona natives, completed their novitiate and made religious profession at Mount St. Joseph. As a result, as Mother Gonzaga's time as provincial came to an end, the decision was made to discontinue the western province, and from 1890 to 1900 the Arizona and California houses became a part of the St. Louis Province. The ministry of the Sisters of St. Joseph in the west, however, continued to grow and spread into surrounding states.

Sisters at the provincialate. Seated from left Sisters Clara Otero, Frances Makey, Priscilla O'Keefe, Elizabeth Parrott, Stanislaus Vedder, Rose Mary Murphy, Mary John Noli. Standing in first row Sisters Clementine Joseph Slattery, Catalina Acosta, Liobe Quintanilla, Marie de Lourdes Le May, Nazaria Day, Ladislaus Duggan, Ludwina Reno. Top row from left Sisters Gabilla Harrigan, Edna Stone, Aurelia Mary Doyle.

CHAPTER 3

SERVING ON THE INDIAN MISSIONS

"In memory we honor and bless those sisters who lived with and loved the Indians they cared for, and who worked so long and so hard with difficulties and privations we can neither imagine nor understand."

–Alberta Cammack, CSJ

Beginning with the 1873 foundation at the Papago mission in San Xavier del Bac, requests for sisters to start schools for Indians came more and more frequently. In 1886, Reverend Mother Agatha Guthrie received a request from Rev. J.A. Stephan, director of the Bureau of Catholic Indian Missions, for sisters to take over the government school at Fort Yuma. Aware of the violent and rebellious history of the Yumas and of the failure of civilizing efforts of the military and of the school staff they were being asked to replace, Mother Agatha at first refused the request. She feared, too, that the sisters would not be allowed to teach religion in the school and to have access to the spiritual support of a chaplain. Eventually, assured that the sisters would be free to teach religion to the children and would receive the full support of the school superintendent, she reluctantly gave her permission. Her premonitions proved to be accurate when after the sisters experienced years of success in their loving work with the Yumas, they met threats and obstacles that eventually forced their withdrawal.

Mother Julia Littenecker, assistant general superior, traveled to Yuma in March with Mother Ambrosia O'Neil, the future superior and administrator, to wait for the transfer of the school to the sisters' jurisdiction. The transfer did not take place until May 1, so they

Chief Pasqual, Yuma, Arizona

spent their time getting acquainted with the situation and with the Indians. They learned that the Yumas were pagan, lacking the Christian heritage that the Papagos at San Xavier del Rey had brought to the sisters' school. But the Yuma's Chief Pasqual was a wise leader who had taught his people to avoid lying, cheating, and drinking. Mother Julia described her first meeting with Pasqual: "We went yesterday across the bridge to see Chief Pasqual. He received us with marks of great respect and kissed our hands. The Indians were looking on in astonishment... Himself and his squaw were dressed in Adam's fashion; so are the generality of the Yumas." [1]

After a period of observation, Pasqual came to trust the sisters. He told them that "he would do his part toward us; that if we came to do them good, he would be good to us, and would also teach his people to be good to us; that hitherto many fine promises had been made to him and his people by persons sent by the Government, but these were not carried out." He not only urged, but commanded his tribesmen to send their children to the school because the sisters "were from God and would bring good to the tribe." [2]

The fort school opened on May 5, 1886 with 59 pupils and numbers increasing every day. Mother Julia wrote that "Pasqual had told the Indians that they must all send their little ones to the Sisters – they will learn more easily, because their heads are yet tender. As for the big boys and girls he fears their heads are already too hard to learn." After a week of progress, Mother Julia reported: "They knew nothing of English when we commenced last week; and now, they know by heart how to make the Sign of the Cross, the Our Father, and the fundamentals of the Catechism. They are fond of singing, (though I assure you, they had never been used to anything except wild yells.)"

The sisters loved and cared for the Yumas. Sr. Alphonse described the living conditions of her Yumas. "There is not an hour some poor Yuma is not coming to tell how sick they are. It would make your heart ache to see them, sick, suffering, and hungry, and to visit them in their camps to see how they live and what they have to eat—you would be surprised that more of them are not sick. We go every week away in the Reservation to see the sick." Reverend Mother must have been amused at one of Mother Julia's letters. "Sister Alphonse was asked yesterday to prescribe for a new patient—the Chief's horse. She ordered something that she thought would do the animal good, and he was all right afterwards. She has quite a reputation already."

Chief Pasqual was soon drawn to the faith of the sisters and received instructions in Catholicism during the first year. In May 1887, Mother Ambrosia wrote to Mother Julia: "Last Sunday we celebrated the anniversary of our opening the Yuma school and on that day also we had poor old Chief Pasqual baptized. He has been failing fast for some time past." Fr. Chaucot baptized Pasqual on May 1, "but poor old Pasqual was not able to come to the chapel, so Father baptized him in his room. There were three or four Yumas present." On May 9, "our dear Lord called him home."

With the loss of Pasqual's wise leadership, the sisters began to experience opposition to their work at the fort. Pasqual's son Miguel became chief of the Yumas and proved to be such a poor leader that he was deposed in May 1893. Encouraged by a small faction of bitterly hostile anti-Catholics in Yuma, Miguel blamed the sisters, and particularly Mother Ambrosia, for his disgrace. "Miguel was determined to be reinstated, but was convinced this could not be effected as long as the sisters were at the Fort. If 'El Capitan' (the Indian boys' favorite name for Mother Ambrosia) could be done away with, the other sisters would leave and Miguel would once more be chief." [3]

Miguel planned the murder for the night of October 27, 1893, "but Mother Ambrosia, because of the suspicious actions of Miguel's followers, stationed two Sisters in each building with the children. All remained awake awaiting the attack which might occur at any moment. Several times during the night the murderers came as far as the convent door but retreated each time. Towards morning a

Christian Yuma led Mother Ambrosia and her companions to a hiding place below the hill. Shortly after, the horde stormed the convent only to be overpowered by a guard of faithful Indians who had secretly entered and were awaiting the attackers. Miguel and his followers were brought to trial and served prison sentences at Los Angeles." [4]

The sisters continued to staff the school at the fort for another seven years, but experienced increasing prejudice by the government against religious employed in government schools. Finally, a newly appointed superintendent of the school began to prevent Mother Ambrosia from exercising her leadership role in the school, and to actively interfere with the religious activities of the sisters, preventing their access to the Indians and finally removing their chaplain. With their work blocked at every turn, Reverend Mother Agatha formally withdrew the sisters from Fort Yuma in spring 1900.

Eighteen years before the sisters left the Yuma Indian mission, Sisters of St. Joseph were establishing a school in San Diego, thanks to the persevering requests of Fr. Antonio Ubach, zealous missionary for the Indians of the Southwest. A native of Spain, he was in San Diego by 1866 as pastor of the huge parish which stretched from the Pacific Ocean to the Colorado River. His consuming goal soon became to provide Catholic education for the children of the Southwest, particularly for his Indians. What he needed was a committed group of teachers.

Then, in the spring of 1870, he met the Sisters of St. Joseph when the original seven were in San Diego making arrangements for a wagon and driver to take them to Tucson. Impressed with these sisters and their courage, he continually made requests to Reverend Mother Agatha Guthrie to send sisters to San Diego to found a school, even making the long trip to Carondelet, Missouri, to plead for help. Reverend Mother denied the requests, thinking that San Diego was too far away. "In his disappointment, he told of his thirty days of Masses and his confidence in St. Joseph, who had never before failed him. The superior general was much affected by the priest's faith in the power of St. Joseph and answered, 'This request must have come directly from our Holy Patron, and the Sisters of St. Joseph will open your school in far away San Diego.'" [5]

The first group of sisters arrived in 1882 and established a day school for girls and boys in San Diego, naming it after Our Lady of Peace. As this school prospered, "Ubach renewed his twenty year effort to secure a government contract for an industrial (vocational) school. He was increasingly concerned about 'the Indian children that roam in our streets' and he fought the 'repugnant trade' of Indian girls for the horses and livestock of the white ranchers." [6] After much effort, Fr. Ubach finally received a government contract for a mission school in San Diego's Old Town for fifty children with a stipend of $12.50 a month for each child to cover buildings, education, clothing, and food. Sisters Hyacinth Blanc and Teresa Ortiz opened the school in 1887, driving a horse and buggy every day from their convent at Our Lady of Peace. In honor of Fr. Ubach's patron saint, the school was named St. Anthony's Industrial School for Indians.

As St. Anthony's prospered and grew, Fr. Ubach began plans to relocate the school to the site of the abandoned Mission San Diego de Alcala six miles east in the valley. The mission, founded by Fr. Junipero Serra in 1769, had been staffed by the Franciscans until 1834 when the Mexican government took over the property from church ownership. Abandoned now by the government, the property had been neglected and needed extensive repair, but Fr. Ubach saw the advantages of the new location. "My facilities in the future for teaching Indian pupils industrial pursuits, such as farming, gardening, stock raising, dairy work, and shoemaking, will be ample and complete, as I have some two hundred acres of fine land belonging to the Old Mission which over 123 years ago was destined and used for this very same purpose!" [7] Classes began at the mission

St. Anthony's Indian School, San Diego, founded by Fr. Antonio Ubach

at the end of October 1891, and Fr. Ubach said the first Mass on November 1, the Feast of All Saints. Sr. Archangela reported that this was the first Mass said on the famous spot since the Franciscans left it. [8]

St. Anthony's averaged about 90 to 100 boys and girls in the 1890s, supported almost totally by the modest government stipends. Children were trained in agriculture, shoe-making, sewing and domestic work. The school's curriculum was thorough, as a child's letter published in the *Mission Indian* shows: "I am in the fourth grade. I study grammar, physiology, spelling, catechism, Bible history, geography and arithmetic. I am trying to do the best I can. I am very glad to be here with the Sisters. They are very kind to us. We have mass every morning." [9]

In 1900, the United States government ceased all appropriations for Indian contract schools, forcing the Bureau of Catholic Indian Affairs to take over the support of all Indian schools, an almost impossible task. St. Anthony's financial struggles became more and more acute. When Fr. Ubach died in 1907, St. Anthony's was able to continue for less than a year. "Almost immediately, the Indians felt the loss of their beloved champion, and those who lived close to San Diego sadly gathered their families about them and moved quietly back into the lands farther away from the white man and his ways." By 1908 there were so few children left at the Old Mission that they were taken to St. Boniface Indian School in Banning, California. [10]

In 1888, a year after the founding of St. Anthony's School in San Diego, the Sisters of St. Joseph were able to return to their beloved Papagos at San Xavier del Bac, the "White Dove of the Desert" south of Tucson. San Xavier had been their first Indian mission, begun in 1873 three years after they arrived in Tucson, and always close to their hearts. The mission had been without a government agent or any provision for education since the sisters had had to withdraw in 1876, and almost all trace of civilization and education had been lost. When Bishop Bourgade, Salpointe's successor, begged the sisters to return to San Xavier, the congregation saw the critical need and, although aware that there would be no government support and no possibility of funds from the diocese, accepted the bishop's request.

Three sisters came down the old mission road once again to

resume their ministry to the Papagos. Mother Florence Benigna O'Reilly, Sisters Agnes Orosco and Bernadette Smith found the mission in ruinous condition. There was no question of opening a school or serving the Indian people until the buildings were cleared out. The sisters set to work with shovels and buckets, hauling out load after load of rubble and bat droppings. "Pans of burning sulfur were set out to fumigate the rooms, and each sister armed with a broom attacked scorpions, centipedes, and other crawling creatures as they dropped from the ceiling and walls." Within a few months, an exhausted Mother Florence was replaced by Mother Aquinas Duffy who was to remain at the mission for more than forty years. Once the schoolrooms were clean and ready for occupancy, the sisters went around the reservation coaxing the children to come to school. "The little ones came to school without shoes or stockings. The girls wore cheap calico dresses; the boys, shirts of flour sack material. For those who came to school hungry, the sisters gave them food out of their own meager portions." [11]

In their time outside school, the sisters studied the Papago

Schoolchildren in front of San Xavier del Bac

dialect, and began to visit Indians in their mud and straw huts called "wickiups". Mother Aquinas describes the experience of visiting the Indians in their homes to care for the sick and assist at death beds. "In order to seek admittance into one, it was necessary to crawl in through a little opening near the ground, which was neither easy nor agreeable. It was so dark when inside that it was necessary to feel until you found the sick person." [12]

As the sisters gradually made progress in educating the children and teaching the families basic habits of cleanliness and work, their greatest hardship was the lack of a resident chaplain. A priest from Tucson came out on the second and fourth Sundays and on Thursdays to offer the Holy Sacrifice of the Mass. On the first and third Saturdays the horse and wagon was sent from St. Mary's Hospital to take the sisters in to Tucson for Mass, a trip that took almost all day. They returned the next day with their wagon loaded with provisions. It was a long time before the sisters were able to have their own chapel at the mission, a little room in the tower of the church, for their own prayer in the presence of the Blessed Sacrament.

As the years passed, life on the reservation was transformed. The mission began to receive some support from the government in 1910. Many Indians were baptized and educated in the faith. "The

San Xavier del Bac

men and women were persuaded to give up their games and instead till the soil and care for their homes and families. The Sisters became not only the teachers, but also the doctors, nurses, the spiritual advisers of the whole reservation. It was they who, in the absence of the priest, closed the eyes of the dying Indian and officiated at his funeral. At their insistence and encouragement, the women were taught what should have been instinctively theirs, the art of molding pottery and weaving baskets." [13]

The work of the sisters continued at San Xavier until 1932 when the government withdrew its support from the Mission. Neither the diocese nor the congregation was able to support continuing the school, and the Sisters of St. Joseph reluctantly had to withdraw.

Another boarding school for Indians opened in 1889 in Banning, in the lovely California valley between the San Jacinto and San Bernardino mountains. With the support of the Sr. Katherine Drexel foundation, Monsignor Joseph Stephan, director of the Bureau of Catholic Indian Missions, purchased eighty acres of land in Banning and built a school which included a large three-story building, other small buildings, an outdoor shrine and a small church. Knowing well the work of the Sisters of St. Joseph, Monsignor Stephan once again asked Reverend Mother Agatha to send sisters to Banning.

While negotiations with the Sisters of St. Joseph were going on, the school enrolled its first students in 1889. Fr. Florian Hahn, of the Congregation of the Precious Blood, became superintendent of the school. Six sisters of St. Joseph—Mother Celestia Reilly, Sisters Anna Francis Stack, Alphonse Lamb, Gonzaga Covey, Virginia Joseph Byrne, and Lydia Bulger—arrived in time for the opening of school on September 1, 1890.

With government support promised for 100 students, St. Boniface accepted 120 students that fall, regretfully having to refuse fifty more. The school was immediately successful, offering reading, writing, arithmetic, religion, good citizenship, music and sports. The boys were trained in trades with a specialty in farming and gardening; the girls learned household arts, bead and lace work.

The children's parents were unable to pay, and seldom able to visit. These were families who lived in the desert and high in the mountains as far south as San Diego and the Mexican border. Few of them could even come to pick up their children for summer vacation. So a trek began every spring, with as many as fifteen farm wagons filled with children led by Fr. Hahn, driving a supply wagon drawn by a team of horses, and Sisters Anna Frances Stack and Thomas Lavin riding in a buggy—"de luxe" in Sr. Anna Frances' term. When the children arrived at their villages, the caravan was welcomed with enthusiasm and a little feast. Before leaving, Fr. Hahn would always say Mass and hear confessions.

When the Drexel money had to be withdrawn because of the increasing number of Mother Katherine's own mission foundations, and government support dwindled away, the struggling school received increasing support from the Catholic people of California, under the leadership of Bishops Thomas Conaty and John J. Cantwell. The hard work of the sisters and children also contributed to the school's income. Sr. Mary Anne Bahner, missioned at Banning in the early 1930s, remembered: "We had 150 Indian children who lived there twelve months a year. They ate mostly beans donated by Oxnard farmers, also fruit—apricots which we picked, dried and canned. After Mother Katherine Drexel withdrew her support we existed on the proceeds of a barbecue festival held every year....The sisters worked very hard. With the children we did all the laundry. The boys under a male director, Tom Southam, tended the pigs and milked the cows."

Fr. Hahn died in 1916 and eventually his place was filled by Franciscan priests. St. Boniface School gradually changed from an Indian school to a shelter for troubled children and wards of the juvenile courts. When in 1953, Precious Blood School was established in the town of Banning, classes were discontinued out at the Indian School, which was taken over by the San Diego diocese as a boys' school. Three years later, the sisters of St. Joseph left St. Boniface to staff Precious Blood School closing sixty-six years of service to the St. Boniface Indian children.

The fifth Arizona Indian school where the sisters served was by common agreement the poorest, the driest, and the hottest. St. John's Mission School in Komatke, southwest of Phoenix, was opened by Franciscan fathers in 1900, and by 1901 Reverend Mother Agatha was agreeing to send sisters to the school. Sisters Anna de Sales Power and St. Barbara Reilly set out from Tucson by train, crossing an unstable bridge over the swollen Gila River by handcar. Joined by

Sr. Anna de Sales

The CSJ who ministered the longest in Komatke was Sr. Anna de Sales, the New York-born girl who entered the convent, but was prevented three times by her family from receiving the habit. She finally went to St. Louis to continue her religious life, never dreaming that of her 67 years in that life she would spend fifty as a pioneer in Arizona—Yuma, San Xavier, and Komatke.

Sr. Anna de Sales and two companions came to Komatke in the hottest part of the desert, in the hottest month of year, at the hottest time of day. Later, she commented how providential it had been that when reverend mother had asked the provincial to see what kind of place Komatke was, a terrible storm had turned the inquirers back. Otherwise, the sisters would probably not have been allowed to go there. One of the Franciscan fathers stated that Komatke was the most arduous of all missions, the work there requiring heroic souls.

Only six days after the pioneer sisters had arrived, they opened school with 120 pupils but no classrooms. In the church, Father put up temporary partitions which had to be taken down every Friday. Mother Anna and Sr. St. Barbara taught the first grade which consisted of grown-up men down to little toddlers hardly able to step up to the door.

In the early days, meals consisted of bread and beans. Before 1907, the sisters and older girls got up at 3:00 a.m. to make tortillas for the children's breakfast, baking them on tripods out in the yard. On rainy days, umbrellas were held over the workers. After 1907, the bread was baked in a crude homemade oven built of adobe, stone, and brick. The dough was set in the evening. At 3:00 a.m., Mother Anna de Sales and two big boys kneaded the dough for rising, formed it into loaves and baked them.

By the time World War I broke out, there were 450 children, all being well cared for. When the Indian men joined the war, the food supply became scarce. One morning there was nothing for the evening meal and no prospects of getting anything. Mother Anna de Sales took seven beans over to the church, told Our Lord there was nothing for the children and to please hurry up and find some food for them. She left the seven beans at the foot of St. Joseph's statue. "Father went into town while we all prayed. Late in the afternoon, we saw the mission wagon coming slowly over the desert road. Our spirits were cheered as we knew and felt God would not forget us. As Father drove in, we saw the wagon was well-packed with beans and potatoes."

Although the sisters endured days of hardship and struggle, they were full of joy and contentment. Mother Anna de Sales, who was always able to see the funny side of things, was a source of encouragement. One young woman who visited often from Phoenix described her: "the tiny figure in a CSJ habit with her bright happy smile...She would say with such love in her voice, 'They are so shy.' But they were never shy with her. I saw the oldest and most weather-beaten men in the tribe kneel at her feet and receive her blessing...She was Irish to the core, the ever-merry twinkle in her blue eyes."

Constance Fitzgerald, CSJ

Sr. Mary Joseph Franco in Phoenix, the three traveled the eighteen miles to the mission by buggy through the August desert heat.

When they arrived at the mission, they found a small adobe convent and a church which doubled as school during the week. Alone, the sisters inspected their little home. The boxes they had sent ahead were stacked on the dirt floor. Sr. Anna de Sales recollected the scene: "We then and there began to adjust ourselves to whatever we had. Two of us began moving and opening boxes and as we moved the different boxes the scorpions thought best to move. Of course we did not allow them to go very far. As we were accustomed to their movements from our experiences on other Indian missions we procured a couple of good sized sticks and as each came in sight, dispatched them." Sister Mary Joseph summed up their feelings as they began to settle in, "Thank God, we are home!" [14]

One hundred and twenty pupils, ranging from six to 18 years old, appeared for the first day of school. "The children responded very faithfully to studying and learned many hymns and songs which pleased the parents very much," Sister Anna de Sales reported. "Each year more pupils came. By 1908 we had 375 children." Because the Indians' homes were scattered far across the surrounding desert, the pastor, Fr. Justin Deutsch, recognized the need for a boarding school, and built two huts of sticks and mud which served as girls' and boys' dormitories.

Sr. Euphrasia Marin with Komatke music-makers

Probably the greatest hardship at St. John's was lack of good drinking water. "The only water available at the mission was alkaline, tasting bitterly of common salt mixed with potassium salt. Besides being distasteful for drinking purposes, it withered any kind of vegetation; hence there could be no mission gardens or trees of any kind." It was many years before a visitor from the Catholic Indian Bureau saw the problem and raised enough money to sink a well on the property. [15]

In the early days, cooking was done outside in big pots. The children had their dinner in the girls' house which had many uses as Sister Anna de Sales writes. We used the girls' house "for a dining room by spreading a cloth on the floor and this was the table. We used it also for dormitory and recreation hall. Each child brought a blanket from home. After supper each one of the 40 or 50 children that we had boarding spread out the blanket very carefully on the dirt floor after saying night prayers, lay down on the ground and rolled themselves in the blanket for the night."

Laundry day was just as simple. Since each child had no change of clothing, they were draped in aprons or shawls and sent to sit in the sun while the sisters and the older girls washed the clothes in the river and hung them on bushes to dry. "Their clothes dried quickly in this dry climate, so it did not take long and the children all had clean clothes on and were as happy as if clothed in silk."

Aware of the poverty of the mission, sisters throughout the congregation, as well as friends in nearby Phoenix, sent clothes and gifts and statues for the church. Sister Mary Joseph wrote to Reverend Mother in 1904, "The two trunks came with everything you sent for our children....Dear mother, you have no idea how glad we were to get those little

Sr. Mary Joseph Franco with the grandchild of Chief Geronimo

shirts and overalls. We have so many poor children whose parents are too poor to clothe….As for the big suits they just came in good time. The black one I am going to keep for a poor old man that's very anxious to make his First Communion, but the other evening he came to tell me that he is afraid he could not make it because he did not have a nice suit. We have a class of old people who are to make their First Communion about Christmas. I wish you could be here. It is a sight worth seeing. How earnest they are, and how well they try to prepare for this beautiful occasion. What grand faith they have."

As the years went by, additional buildings were erected and larger numbers of students could be received. The plant took on the proportions of a small village, and by 1922 the resident students numbered 500 boys and girls who enjoyed the ordinary conveniences of civilized life in food, clothing, shelter, and a liberal education, not omitting championships in athletics. "Where a small group of children used to sit on the ground and partake of one or two messes of brown beans daily with a possible serving of meat once a month, these five hundred were served at table, three meals daily; milk and bread and meat and vegetables with occasional luxuries such as fruit and cookies."

The Sisters of St. Joseph served at St. John's mission in Komatke for 37 years until the withdrawal of Drexel funds made it necessary for them to leave the mission. Sr. Anna de Sales's words expressed the feelings of many sisters who had spent years working with their dear Indians. "I often ask myself what good did I ever do that God so favored me to be here."

Pioneers of Komatke mission with Fr. Justin Deutsch, OFM. From left Sr. Barbara Reilly, Mother Anna de Sales Power, Sr. Mary Joseph Franco

CHAPTER 4

CALIFORNIA FOUNDATIONS

"They were as surely pioneers as the people who came in the earlier days."

Adele Koop, OLP 1894

The decision in 1890 to discontinue the western province may have seemed like a setback for the little group of sisters in Arizona and California, but the work of ministry continued unchecked. In the decades following, St. Mary's Hospital and the schools in Tucson and Prescott flourished. San Xavier, Yuma, San Diego, Banning, and Komatke continued to serve the Indian population so dear to the sisters, and California ministries expanded in Los Angeles, San Diego, Oakland, Oxnard, and San Francisco.

Recognizing the healthy growth of ministry in the west, the General Chapter of 1899 passed a unanimous vote to reinstate the Western Province, but to change the location of the provincial house. Mother Mary Elizabeth Parrot was appointed provincial and established temporary headquarters at St. Joseph's Academy on 15th and 6th in Tucson as she began a search for a permanent center for the province. For the next three years, Mother Mary Elizabeth and Mother Julia Littenecker, assistant general, studied the areas of ministry of the sisters, visited the houses of the western province, and prayerfully considered the options. Finally, the decision was made to situate the provincial house at St. Mary's Academy, in Los Angeles, California.

It was a prudent choice, opting for California which had been a state since 1850, rather than for the still developing territory of

Arizona. As the new century began, California was experiencing rapid population growth, particularly in the south of the state. Los Angeles "had its own particular evolution. Irrigation made intensive cultivation, especially of citrus fruits, possible. Great oil deposits and cheap electric power brought rapid industrial expansion. Shipping and commerce were attracted by a man-made harbor." [1] Despite the size of the state, the developing railroad systems made transportation available and relatively inexpensive.

Probably the most important element in the decision to move the province center to Los Angeles was the large and growing Catholic population there. "In the first decade of the twentieth century the percentage of Catholics in the total population of the Monterey-Los Angeles diocese was one to six." There were large colonies of immigrants of diverse cultures, in addition to the English-speaking people and the rapidly growing Mexican and Spanish population. Led by two strong and visionary bishops—Bishop George Montgomery and Bishop Thomas J. Conaty—churches, schools, and social services were developing rapidly. [2]

The move of the provincialate to St. Mary's received the approval of the Church during the visit of the apostolic delegate to the United States to St. Mary's Academy, May 1, 1903. Mother Mary Elizabeth took up her official residence at St. Mary's in November 1903, and Bishop Conaty officiated at the first reception of postulants on March 19, 1904. The next month, Mother Clotilda McCormick arrived from St. Louis and was installed as mistress of novices, the beginning of a long and loving

St. Mary's Academy on 21st and Grand, Los Angeles, third location of the provincialate and novitiate

term of service. Numbers of young women entering the novitiate increased, and the Sisters of St. Joseph were soon able to support and expand the already thriving ministries of the province.

St. Mary's Academy had been educating young people in Los Angeles a decade before it became the center of the province. In 1868, two years before the sisters arrived in Tucson, Bishop Thaddeus Amat, bishop of the diocese of Monterey-Los Angeles, wrote to Mother St. John Facemaz asking for sisters for his diocese. A year earlier, the bishop, a member of the Vincentian order, had established St. Vincent's College for Boys in Los Angeles. With no sisters available to be sent, Mother St. John could not respond to his needs. But California stayed in the minds of the Carondelet leadership. In 1884, Mother Agatha Guthrie wrote to Amat's successor, Bishop Francis Mora, saying that the community was able now to supply teachers for a school.

Bishop Amat's dream was finally realized when a correspondence began in 1888 between Mother Agatha and Fr. Aloysius Meyer, president of St. Vincent's College for Boys, and plans were made for the sisters to open a school in Los Angeles. From the beginning, the intent was to have both a parish school and an academy for girls. Fr. Meyer wrote: "I agree with you in calling the school an academy, for besides there being a great deal in a name, your school will be it in reality; we must also consider it a parish school, where all the girls in the parish can go, even, as you so kindly mention, the poor, for we must never neglect them; otherwise the Lord would not bless us, and besides we must have room for our little boys." The original land where the first academy was built was signed over to the congregation with the provision that the sisters would always provide for a parish school at St. Vincent's.[3]

Reverend Mother Agatha made the long train trip to Los Angeles bringing sisters for the new school. They arrived on the Feast of the Epiphany, January 6, 1889, and traveled from the train station by horse and buggy several miles beyond the city to 21st and Grand where their new home was waiting for them. Classes began the next day with 65 pupils.

Southern California in the middle of the winter must have been a wonder to the sisters from the Midwest. Sr. Teresa Louise Crowley, Mother Agatha's companion on the trip, asked Fr, Meyer what the chief industry was in California. "After a long pause he replied – Climate." She wrote back to St. Louis several days later. "The house is beautifully built—rooms large, ceilings high, plenty of light. In the middle of the day one does not need red flannels, but summer ones are very comfortable…The dew is very heavy which accounts for the penetrating cold but the trees and the flowers…everything is so bewitching that one cannot help feeling herself in the land of the Angels in every deed. I am happy as the day is long. Well, if I were in the world, I'd be willing to work ten years in the land of blissards [sic] and then come here to spend my money." Reverend Mother was so taken with the climate that, wanting to bring a piece of it home with her, she sent a trunk full of grape vines and another filled with dried fruit. "The trunks were sent today on our tickets and will be at the Depot when you receive this letter. Trunk is full of Grape vines with the Roots and I fear they will be frozen if Sr. Victorine don't get them soon."

There are many fond recollections of the early years at St. Mary's Academy. Judith M. Furlong, who enrolled at St. Mary's in 1895, remembered the simple frame building of 324 W. 21st Street with its meager furnishings. "It was the horse and buggy age. The milk carts clattered down the streets at 2 A.M. and weary drivers hurried home with the dawn, but one I remember, Thomas Conneally, always stopped for Mass at St. Vincent's and as he passed the school, somehow he always had a few extra qts. of milk to leave….As special treat we were allowed to drive the Sisters out on Sunday afternoon in a fringed-top surrey with a pair of golden sorrels, of which some of the sisters were mortally afraid." [4]

As enrollment at St. Mary's Academy grew, a new wing was added with space for the provincial offices, novitiate and a new chapel, and two houses purchased for classrooms, a music department, and resident students quarters. Sr. Dolorosa Mannix, teacher at St. Mary's, recollects that "the peaceful neighborhood did not require precautions. Sr. Louis and Sr. Dolorosa who roomed in 'Brown's house' left both front and back door open at night."

But soon St. Mary's and the province outgrew the cluster of buildings on 21st and Grand, and the search began for a new location for the Academy. In 1904 a twenty-acre site southwest of the city was purchased. Construction of the new St. Mary's Academy and provincialate, as described by historian Sr. Lucida Savage, following the "Spanish Mission style, embodied the best traditions of that form of architecture....deep arcades, flower-filled patios, and pergolas in the midst of tropical gardens." The chapel was designed by Tiffany Studios of New York.[5]

The new St. Mary's was finally ready in the summer of 1911, and the sisters moved in on July 16. Sr. Laurentine Falvey, a postulant that year, shared her memory of the move. "We postulants were told to have [our] suitcases packed and to assemble on the porch of the Kays House....We were there when we received another order to go back to the novitiate. We went and Mother Clotilda told us we had been accepted to receive the holy habit. She walked with us...to the

St. Mary's Academy on Slauson and Crenshaw, fourth site of Los Angeles province center

corner of 22nd and Grand Avenue...where the electric car stopped. We boarded the car, paid our five cents and were on our way to the new St. Mary's at Slauson Ave. and Mesa Drive. It was a wide open location there [with] large vegetable gardens....and cattle grazing. The 5-cent ride on our carline went only as far as the car barns. We took our suitcases and carried them through these gardens....Parts of the gardens had been freshly irrigated so we reached Slauson with wet, muddy shoes and our black skirts well soaked and mud-spattered."

Despite their careful planning and vision, the sisters' move to their new site met some criticism. Many people commented that it was foolish of the sisters to build in such an isolated area, well outside the city. Transportation would be difficult because the only streetcar passing the site was an interurban car which ran once an hour. But Mother Catherine Beavers, St. Mary's directress, persuaded the transit directors to run the yellow car as far as the new school, to arrive at 8:30 a.m. and again at 3:30 p.m. With an additional flourish, the transit company built a station in the style of the academy, stucco and red tile, and marked it "St. Mary's Academy"![6]

St. Mary's station

With the establishment of St. Mary's Academy and provincialate in southwest Los Angeles, the sisters had laid one more important foundation of their ministry in the western province. But this was not the first time Sisters of St. Joseph had opened a school in California. When Father Antonio Ubach finally

St. Mary's Academy

succeeded in bringing the sisters to San Diego in 1882, he had no way of knowing that in addition to starting a school and a home for Indian children, he was laying the foundation for the Academy of Our Lady of Peace, the oldest and still operating secondary school for women south of San Francisco.

On April 18, 1882, seven years before St. Mary's Academy began, four sisters of St. Joseph arrived in San Diego, led by Mother Ambrosia O'Neill. By May 10, they had established a convent and school in a small house on the corner of Second and G Streets, and were conducting their first day of classes with 28 girls and 2 boys. Fifty dollars from Fr. Ubach, supplemented later with tuition and contributions from townspeople, helped the sisters get the school started. Rent was $15 a month, later raised to $20; monthly rental of a piano was $6. Their first Mass was celebrated on June 13 in the tiny chapel which was dedicated to Our Lady of Peace. This simple beginning was the first CSJ foundation in California.

Within two years, the sisters began to look for another location for their rapidly growing school. With the help of $650 received from the generalate and other generous contributions, including $488.25 from the miners of Cuyamaca, they purchased a block of land on Third Avenue and A Street and moved the school in 1885. For the next 40 years on Third and A, along with the young city of San Diego, Our Lady of Peace grew and prospered.

A 1924 brochure for the Academy gives a flavor of these early days in private education.

> *"A boarding and day school for girls and young ladies. The course of instruction embraces every useful and necessary branch of education. It proposes a carefully graded system of studies, beginning with the rudiments of every branch. At their entrance pupils are examined and classified according to their abilities and previous attainment."*

Instruction at Our Lady of Peace was similar to that at the two academies in Tucson and Prescott, St. Mary's Academy in Los Angeles, and other schools being developed by the sisters. A manual for the best methods and courses, written by experienced teachers in

St. Louis in 1884, was put in the hands of each sister teacher to ensure the excellence in education that every child deserved. To balance the rigorous curriculum and to complete the picture of a well-rounded education, the young ladies at Our Lady of Peace were reminded that "refinement of manner and graceful presence are the charm of the cultured woman—hence, every effort is made to induce pupils to acquire one and the other."

By 1923 when Mother St. Catherine Beavers returned to Our Lady of Peace for her second term as superior, she saw that it was time to look for a new location for the Academy. San Diego was rapidly moving out over the hills and canyons, and the school was now downtown. A search for suitable property began, a purchase made, and plans were being made for building "when a very quiet little priest rang the doorbell one early afternoon. He asked to see Mother Catherine. 'Tell her,' he said, 'it is important. I won't keep her a minute if she is not interested.' Mother Catherine sent word that she was busy, but the priest repeated, 'It is just so important that I see her.' Persuaded, Mother Catherine came downstairs and received Fr. [Noel] Sullivan in the fine old parlor. He had heard of a piece of property overlooking Mission Valley that had fallen into the hands of a trust company. Mother consented to accompany him to look at it simply because, as she said, 'I can't refuse him.'" [7]

The property she saw that day was the Vandruff Estate on Copley and Oregon Streets, about 20 acres beautifully located on the Mission Palisades with a view of the valley and the sea. Already on the property were Italian Renaissance buildings, a swimming pool, and elegant terraces and gardens. "Mother St. Catherine returned with a new determination gleaming in her eyes. Reverend Mother Agnes Rossiter, superior general, was holding visitation in the west, and was, at the time, in Los Angeles. The next morning, Mother St. Catherine boarded the train for Los Angeles and returned that evening with Reverend Mother. Proceedings began the very next day." [8]

The California Province received permission from Rome to borrow $200,000 for the purchase and development of the property, but their plans were opposed by a difficult lawsuit. "Long distance calls up and down the coast kept the wires buzzing. The struggle reached its climax the night of January 25, 1924, and the Sisters

Academy of Our Lady of Peace, San Diego

spent that night in vigil. Their prayers were answered, and the following morning *The San Diego Union* carried the triumphant news, 'Catholic Sisters Acquire Vandruff Property As Site for New Academy.'" [9]

Classes began at the new Academy in September 1925. The first Mass was Midnight Mass 1925, celebrated in the new convent chapel; on May 14, 1927, Bishop J.J. Cantwell dedicated and blessed the grounds and buildings.

Just two years after the San Diego sisters started their school on Second and G Streets, Fr. John B. McNally welcomed five sisters to St. Patrick's Parish in Oakland, California. Chartered in 1852, Oakland was a fast-growing railroad terminus on the western edge of the continent. In 1860 its population was 1,543, twenty years later it had reached 34,555. Workers, many of them Irish, crowded into the area to work on the railroads and in the shipyards. St. Patrick's parish, created for the increasing Catholic population, was headed by the colorful and energetic Fr. McNally.

The first thing Fr. McNally did was build a church, tall and impressive. The next most important thing he did was to bring the Sisters of St. Joseph of Carondelet to open a school "for girls and small boys." Three arrived by steamer from San Diego on December 18, 1883, and with some delays because of heavy rains and washouts, Reverend Mother Agatha Guthrie arrived on January 1, bringing two more, including Sr. Florence Benigna O'Reilly, the superior. These five opened St. Joseph's Institute, the second California foundation, on January 1, 1884. The school opened with 200 pupils and grew so rapidly that the pastor began to build almost immediately. Two additional sisters arrived later that January to help with the exploding numbers of students.

Fr. McNally wrote: "Sister Octavia has eighty boys and more flocking in all the time….and thus it goes everywhere—crowded, young ones jammed, wedged together and huddled together….We have good schools; the people believe it. They are flooding us with their children. Your sisters have done hard and noble work and no one appreciates their labors more than I. They are true and brave women." [10] Dealing with a pastor of such high creative energy was a challenge Mother Agatha recognized. She wrote on January 13: "The Sisters here will have to be up and doing to satisfy the requirements of the pastor. He is in class all the time. Gives everything needed for the school and for the comfort of the Sisters but they on their part have to be wide awake….What a thorough young man Fr. Mac is."

She must have enjoyed her correspondence with Fr. Mac. In 1886, he wrote to her: "We are all doing fine work; the St. Joseph Sisters are doing the finest…I must say, they live very near me, and I hear no noise. I think they are quite peaceable and happy, harmonious, pious and entirely consistent. They are getting fat in their new convent, especially Mother Florence. Come and see for yourself. I am getting thin, gone to shadow. Pray for this poor fellow…" [11]

St. Joseph's Institute continued to grow. Classrooms, music rooms, and an auditorium were added. A commercial department began in 1909 with business, clerical and secretarial courses for the older girls.   The school building was renovated and enlarged during the 1931-32 school year, and the name was changed on February 23, 1932 to St. Patrick Elementary School. The Sisters of St. Joseph continued to teach the children of St. Patrick's until 1985, a total of 108 years of CSJ ministry and presence in the parish. Fr. McNally had proudly called the schools in his parish "Schools of the Faith." A report in *The Oakland Tribune* on December 20, 1945 would have given him great joy: "The pastor of St. Patrick's reports that 25 of its young men have entered the priesthood and 53 young women have become sisters." Since the beginnings of St. Joseph's Institute, its graduates have responded to God's call to religious life and have

Senior girls, St. Joseph Institute, 1893

taken their place responsibly as citizens of their world. St. Patrick School formally closed its doors in June 1996, and was succeeded July 1 by a new school—St. Martin de Porres School which was formed from three existing schools—Sacred Heart, St. Columba, and St. Patrick's.

A new ministry came to Oakland in 1894 when Mrs. Margaret McCourtney offered her estate on Telegraph Avenue and 41st Street for the purpose of establishing a school and home for deaf children. Instruction and care of the deaf had been close to the heart of the Sisters of St. Joseph since another generous woman—the Countess de la Rochejacquelin—had financed the journey of the first sisters to America in 1836. Bishop Joseph Rosati had invited the sisters to St. Louis with a particular project in mind—to direct an institute for the deaf that he intended to establish in St. Louis. The school for the deaf that opened in 1838 is still in existence today, and Mrs. McCourtney's sister had been educated there. When she asked Archbishop Riordan's permission for the foundation of the school, she requested that the Sisters of St. Joseph staff the home.

St. Joseph's Home for the Deaf opened on May 13, 1895 with two faculty—Sisters Alphonsus Peters and Rose Catherine Casey who had come from the deaf institute in St. Louis. Enrollment grew so that on the following year they needed to purchase some adjoining property and enlarge the school to add classrooms, dormitories, and a chapel. Mrs. McCourtney died a little over a year after the school opened, leaving her property to the Sisters of St. Joseph. But without an endowment, there was always a problem of funding the home. A constant supporter was Archbishop Riordan through whose efforts the school received many charitable bequests. "Another good friend of the home was the late Rev. Fr. McNally who was the first clergyman to call on [the superior] and give her a word of encouragement. Through his kindly interest came several substantial sums which helped materially in carrying on the good work. The home is dependent upon charity for its support and when an appeal is made the people respond most generously."

The challenges met by these early teachers at St. Joseph's Home for the Deaf were multiple. Teaching methods relied on the most recent theory. An 1895 account mentions that the combined method was used, including lip-reading, speech, manual alphabet, and sign language, but that primary emphasis would be on oral training whenever possible. All approaches required practice, repetition, and unlimited patience. Soon the sisters added religion instruction and were able to develop in the children a love for their religion and devotion during prayers. A primary role for the teachers was giving love and compassion to these children, often unwanted at home. "Reaching adulthood some former pupils still regard any convent of the Sisters of Saint Joseph as their home." [12] As the school became better known, children came from all the western states, British Columbia, Alaska and Hawaii.

The sisters began to do religious education and catechetical instruction for the deaf in Berkeley in 1913 at the request of Archbishop Riordan. When the original building on Telegraph Avenue had to be demolished as a fire hazard in 1939, St. Joseph's Home for the Deaf closed, but religious instruction of the deaf has continued on both sides of San Francisco Bay. The prayer of the sister who wrote in 1895 "may dear St. Joseph send us more children" has been answered with the continuation of CSJ work with the deaf unbroken for many years.

As the century turned to the 1900's, another foundation was made farther south on the California coast. The request came from Fr. John Pujol, pastor of a new parish in the Oxnard valley, for sisters to staff a school. Unlike the other early foundations in coastal California, this school was to be in the center of a fertile agricultural center. Four sisters arrived in Oxnard in late August, 1901, welcomed by Fr. Pujol and Fr. John Laubacher, his recently ordained assistant pastor. Since the school and convent were still being built, the sisters were housed in a small cottage that was moved from a nearby village, christened "St. Joseph's Bird Nest" by the sisters.

Sr. Liboria, who arrived in November of that year, dictated early memories of Oxnard in 1964. "Crowded conditions in the four-room cottage…necessitated using every available space for sleeping quarters at night. Two sisters bedded down in the bathroom. Mother Dominic and Sr. Hortulana slept in a small room across the hall from the chapel and I made the kitchen my bedroom. I became very friendly with the wood stove as floor space was at a premium; and since the nights were cold I probably fared better than my sister companions." She remembered that Sr. Philomena's trunk was utilized as a side table in the kitchen and Sr. Liboria sat on it during meals. When Sunday dinner was ready, Sr. Hortulana hung a portion of her red flannel underwear on the line as a signal to come home.

On September 3, 1901, St. Joseph's Institute began with a co-ed enrollment from one to twelve. With the new school building still unfinished, school opened in a former restaurant near the railway station. "The tables and chairs served as seats and desks. Sr. Philomena taught the first, second, and third grades in one corner; Sr. Esperance, the fourth, fifth, and sixth in another, and Sr. Hortulana taught the seventh, eighth, and High School in the kitchen."[13]

Meanwhile, in the midst of the Oxnard bean fields, the parish completed the construction of the school on Fourth and D Streets. The building, which accommodated both school and convent, was dedicated on November 26, 1901 and opened for classes the following day. Because many of the children had to travel in from their ranches, the Institute accepted both boarding and day students. Sr. Clarissa reminisced about the unique "traffic problems" in this farming community. "Instead of bicycles to be parked, children's horses had stalls at the north end of the yard, and each child was responsible for the care of his horse."

The early days at St. Joseph's Institute had a unique character.

"The country environment, the work in the fields and in the orchards, and the household tasks enkindled a spirit that penetrated the classrooms. Simple recreations and the joys of home life were reflected in the pupils' unsophisticated and co-operative manners. From the beginning the school in Oxnard caused the least material hardship of all the other educational activities of the Sisters of Saint Joseph in California."[14] The early zeal of Fr. Pujol and the generous kindness of Fr. Laubacher, "their true and loyal friend", were complemented by the loving support of the parishioners who kept the sisters' kitchen shelves stocked with produce from their fields and orchards.

Soon after St. Joseph's Institute was founded, Fr. Laubaucher recognized another important educational need with the growth of the Mexican population in Oxnard. Asking the Sisters of St. Joseph to join him in this new enterprise, he established Our Lady of Guadalupe as a free school. It opened on East Seventh Street near the Sugar Beet Company in September 1906 with 48 pupils. The school was directed by a CSJ principal until 1996, and still continues to serve this growing population.

St. Joseph's Institute continued to flourish as it adapted to the growth in Oxnard. Its name was changed to Santa Clara Grammar and High School in 1930. When the high school moved to its new location on Saviers Road in 1951, it separated from the elementary school. It is now part of the Los Angeles Archdiocese network of secondary schools. The Sisters of St. Joseph no longer staff the schools in Oxnard, but they left behind the spirit and tradition of the early founders who started out in the Bird Nest and an old restaurant to establish Catholic education in the Oxnard valley.

As early CSJ schools were settling in to a pattern of growth and service, a tragic earthquake and fire were factors in bringing Sisters of St. Joseph to San Francisco. When Star of the Sea was established as a mission church out west of the city in 1887, those who lived in the heart of the city thought of it as the Outer Lands. Traveling out there, one meandered off into sand dunes and fog. Real growth did not occur until after the 1906 earthquake and fire. "When Fr. Philip O'Ryan was appointed pastor of Star of the Sea Parish in 1908, he found a vast waste of sand dunes stretching from First Avenue to the Pacific Ocean, and from Golden Gate Park to the Presidio....But since the great fire of 1906 had left thousands homeless...many families were settling in the rapidly developing Richmond district. There was no provision for the Catholic education of the children of the newcomers, and one of Father O'Ryan's first acts as pastor was the building of a parish school." [15]

Hearing about the Sisters of St. Joseph from a nearby pastor who had known them in St. Paul, Fr. O'Ryan invited the community to send sisters to staff his new school. The response was quick. Six sisters, under the leadership of Sr. Mary Germaine Miskell, arrived in December 1908 from the provincial house in Los Angeles, opening the school on January 3, 1909 with 137 children in grades 1-7. Firmly believing in the value of Catholic education, Fr. O'Ryan continued to expand the school, opening a high school the next year on the second floor of the elementary school. A separate high school building was in use by 1924, still co-educational until the boys transferred to St. Ignatius High School in 1927, and Star of the Sea became an academy for girls.

Star's first graduating class in 1914 was impressive. Of the ten girls and two boys who graduated on June 19, 1914, three girls went on to the University of California at Berkeley. Kathryn Parker received her degree and returned to Star of the Sea to teach. Mary Moriarty left Berkeley to become Sr. Philip, CSJ, and was a teacher until her early death in 1924. After a few years at Berkeley, Mary Lynch became a sister of St. Joseph, received the name of Sr. Rose de Lima, and later returned to Berkeley to earn her Ph.D. After teaching in CSJ high schools, she was one of the founders of Mount St. Mary's College and finished her career as chair of the Department of Education. Perhaps less illustrious as these women completing degrees in higher education so early in the century, but certainly more famous was another 1914 Star graduate—the actress Gracie Allen.

Fr. O'Ryan had more than one reason for keeping the children in schools within the parish unit. Star of the Sea parish and its flourishing schools became a rich source of vocations to the priesthood and to religious orders for many years. Already by 1919, six young women had become sisters of St. Joseph, and three men were studying for the priesthood. When the parish celebrated its centennial in 1994, Sr. Marcella Holian compiled a list of religious vocations from the parish. She listed 102 Star graduates who had entered and persevered as sisters of St. Joseph from 1914 up to 1972. The names included provincial superiors and novice directors, school and hospital administrators, college professors, a world-renowned biology researcher, an author of mystery novels, and many beloved teachers, nurses, and parish workers. In addition to the CSJs, she mentioned the 32 graduates in other religious communities of women, and many priests including Jesuits and men in other religious orders.

Star of the Sea, 1948. From left Sisters Denyse Commeree, Agnes Marie O'Laughlin, Mary Martha Harrington, Cyril Gaul, Anne Jeannette Pryor, Colette McCann, Catherine Louise LaCoste, Davida Joseph Conlan

From their first home, a small house on Tenth Avenue, the sisters moved into a new convent on January 25, 1913, and finally to an impressive three-story convent on 8th and Geary, built in 1937 and blessed that year by Archbishop John Joseph Mitty. Star became the welcoming house of hospitality for the rest of the century for CSJs teaching and ministering at Star and nearby parishes, studying at the city universities, coming to "the City" to visit their families. Finally, with dropping enrollment, the high school closed in June 1985, but sisters of St. Joseph continued to live and minister in Star of the Sea parish until 2006.

CHAPTER 5

PIONEERS IN THE NORTHWEST

> *"There is a wonderful future for the Church in your beautiful state, and I consider it a privilege to cooperate with you, through our dear Sisters in Lewiston, in the development of that future."*
>
> Mother Agnes Rossiter
> to Daniel Gorman, Bishop of Boise

Another chapter of the pioneering Sisters of St. Joseph began around the turn of the century far to the north of the Arizona and California missions. This time it was initiated in Idaho by Jesuit priests who became collaborators with the sisters in their works of health care, education, and service to the American Indians.

The story begins with Fr. Joseph M. Cataldo, a Jesuit born in Sicily and trained in Louvain, Belgium, who arrived as a missionary in Idaho Territory in October 1865. Asked to open a Catholic mission with the Nez Perce Indians, he began work near Lewiston, a small town at the confluence of the Snake and Clearwater Rivers. He gradually won the friendship of a few Nez Perce, including Chief Slickpoo who gave him a seven-acre plot four miles from Lapwai, east of Lewiston. Here, in 1874, Cataldo built St. Joseph's Mission Church and established his Nez Perce mission.

Fr. Cataldo and his fellow Jesuits at the mission dreamed of establishing a school for the Indian children, and in the 1880s they were able to begin offering some classes in the church. But it was not until 1902 that a school and convent were built for sisters to staff the school.

Meanwhile, two other Jesuits, pastors of St. Stanislaus Parish in Lewiston, had been trying to attract sisters to the town, in critical need of a public hospital. With the support of Alphonsus Glorieux, Bishop of Boise, and George de la Motte, provincial of the Jesuit Rocky Mountain Province, Fr. Michael Meyer made the first attempts, writing to many congregations of women religious to describe the needs. Several communities sent sisters to research the situation, and in 1897 the Sisters of Divine Saviour of St. Mary came from Wisconsin to work with Fr. Meyer on securing land and beginning fundraising for the hospital. However, the project failed because of strenuous neighbor complaints and insufficient funds, and the sisters returned to Wisconsin. [1]

As Fr. Meyer's successor as pastor, Fr. Hubert A. Post continued the search for sisters and received a response from Sr. Aurelia Bracken, at that time a Sister of St. Joseph of Cleveland. Sr. Aurelia traveled to Lewiston in November, 1901, met with Fr. Meyer and agreed to undertake the task of establishing a hospital. But she would need help. Setting out to recruit others to work with her, she attracted sisters from several communities, a few former sisters, as well as some interested lay women, and gathered them into her community which she called the Sisters of St. Joseph. Dressed in religious habits so they could receive a clergy discount in their fare, they traveled by train to Lewiston. Among them were two sisters whose names would be woven into the history of the Idaho sisters—Sr. Angelica Heenan, at the time a postulant with the Sisters of St. Joseph of Tipton, and Sr. Dominica Ryan, a novice "lent" from the

Lewiston's first hospital on Snake River Avenue, 1902

Belvedere Sisters of St. Joseph who ended up ministering in Lewiston and Slickpoo until her death in 1960. [2]

Moving quickly after she and her little band of women arrived in Lewiston on January 1, 1902, Sr. Aurelia secured a small frame house on Snake River Avenue and opened a nine-bed hospital in early February. Patients were housed on the first floor with the sisters living in crowded conditions above. Babies were born, operations performed, medical conditions treated all in that little house. It was obvious that a larger hospital building would be needed very soon.

Before Sr. Aurelia arrived, Fr. Post had bought an academy building from the Visitation sisters intending to turn it into the permanent hospital, but Sr. Aurelia had other plans. Declaring that the academy building was not satisfactory for a proper hospital, she convinced Fr. Post that a new structure should be built and immediately hired an architect to erect a four-story brick building on Normal Hill. Always supportive, the provincial of the Jesuits deeded property on Sixth Street and Fourth Avenue to the sisters for $10.

Sr. Aurelia was a strong and independent woman, ambitious to bring the vision of a public hospital to reality. Construction began on the new hospital building in early summer 1902, just a few months after her arrival. Determined to use only the best materials regardless of distance or cost, she almost immediately incurred a serious debt. With the difficulty in transporting materials from Portland, Seattle and northern Washington and making numerous

St. Joseph Hospital opened February 1903

adjustments initiated by the sisters during construction, the anticipated cost soared and the construction deadline delayed. When construction was finally completed in February 1903, St. Joseph's Hospital moved from the Snake River Avenue house into the new four-story fifty-bed structure.

At the same time, Sr. Aurelia saw the importance of establishing her little group as a religious community. With the support of Fr. Post and the Bishop of Boise, the community was incorporated in the state of Idaho on October 15, 1902 as the Sisters of St. Joseph of Lewiston. Fr. Post undertook to train the sisters which must have been a challenging task with such a mixture of sisters, ex-sisters, and lay women all in religious dress whether they were nuns or not. While most ministered at the hospital, three sisters were sent by Fr. Post to work with the Nez Perce children in Fr. Cataldo's school in Slickpoo.

By the end of 1903, the situation at the hospital had deteriorated. The debt increased daily, Sr. Aurelia had a difficult personality, and the townspeople were disturbed at the behavior of some of the women who, though dressed as nuns, had not been trained to become religious sisters. People were beginning to refer to them as 'bogus nuns' or 'quasi sisters.' The situation came to a head when Fr. Post, with the backing of the bishop and the Jesuit provincial, asked these women and Sr. Aurelia to leave Lewiston. They were gone in one night in March 1904, leaving only two young untrained sisters at the hospital. These two became the total staff—caring for the sick, doing the housekeeping and the laundry, and begging for money at the local mines. They kept a vegetable garden behind the hospital, a few fruit trees, and a cow. There was no money to hire anyone to help them.

More sisters were desperately needed if the hospital was to survive. Fr. Post wrote to communities of Sisters of St. Joseph in all parts of the country and Canada, asking for a loan of three sisters—one to administer the hospital, one to nurse, the third to help train the novices of the little community. The Sisters of St. Joseph of Tipton was the only community who could respond at least in part. Mother Mary Gertrude Moffitt, superior general, sent two sisters to Lewiston—Sr. Mary Borgia Tourscher to administer the hospital and

Sr. Mary de Pazzi McArdle who became director of novices. Sr. Borgia turned out to be an excellent administrator, the situation settled down, and the hospital began to turn around.

Meanwhile, Fr. Cataldo returned to Slickpoo in late 1904 from a mission trip to Alaska to find the three sisters struggling to manage the school. He described them as "three very delicate sisters," one of whom fainted from exhaustion while he was there. "Things being difficult, our Bishop asked my Superior, Rev. Father De la Motte, to send me East for Sisters. I could not get any Sisters, but I got 12 postulants and came back with them." [3]

Fr. Cataldo's trip east was the beginning of the Slickpoo community of St. Joseph sisters. Unsuccessful at first in Philadelphia, he appealed to Archbishop Patrick John Ryan "who suggested that he start a community of the Congregation of St. Joseph in Idaho, giving him also permission to preach…in the two Jesuit parishes in Philadelphia, and asking his promise to take care of any candidates he might obtain….Father Cataldo finally succeeded in securing twelve young ladies, who were willing to sacrifice home, relatives, friends and all those near and dear to them, to labor henceforth for the conversion of souls in the 'Wilds of Idaho.'" [4] Reminiscing years later, Sr. Mary Aloysius Fleming said, "I am one of the Twelve…When Fr. Cataldo remarked at our Sodality meeting that the Indians were intelligent and eager to learn, I felt that God could use me and my sewing skill at the Mission. I volunteered right away. I enjoy the Indian people." [5]

The young women arrived at Slickpoo on November 13, 1904, gratefully welcomed by the three who had been struggling to maintain the mission school—Sisters Angelica Heenan, Mary Loretta Powers, and Loyola Fennimore. Sr. Loyola described the arrival of the "Philadelphians": "None of you can guess our joy on welcoming Father and his postulants. We did not have much to offer; it was [they] who were the gift bearers. The Indians were interested in the girls' Irish accent so different from Father's." [6]

The new little community settled in at Slickpoo. Sr. Angelica was both superior of the group and novice director, although she did not make her perpetual vows until 1906. Fr. Cataldo acted as spiritual advisor and officiated as the twelve received the habit of the Sisters of

St. Joseph on the feast of the Epiphany, January 6, 1905, at St. Joseph's church in Slickpoo. The community flourished and grew as more young women from nearby towns came to join them, even a few more coming from Philadelphia. Cataldo was able to fulfill his promise to Archbishop Ryan, staying until nine of the original group made their first vows on November 13, 1907. Soon after that, he was transferred to another mission.

When Cataldo returned to Slickpoo in 1915, he found that his Indian school was beginning to change. With the encouragement of the bishop, the sisters had taken in a number of orphans to be cared for together with the Indian children. The mission was becoming a joint Indian school and orphanage. Soon after he had come back, the mission, with its wooden structures, had a devastating fire. Just before the school opened in 1916, the mission building was completely destroyed by fire. The eighty-year-old priest, with the help of friends and neighbors, managed to put up temporary structures so that the school could open without delay.[7]

St. Joseph's Children's Home, Slickpoo

Another fire destroyed the buildings again in October 1925 with more devastating results. Six little Indian children lost their lives in the fire, having run back into the burning building to get some of their belongings. Mother Borgia wrote from the Lewiston hospital: "My own dear Reverend Mother, Your kind telegram reached us as we returned from the funeral of our six little victims of the terrible fire, and was like a balm to our hearts. Many thanks for your sympathy....The loss of life was all caused by the children going back into the building by the door at the other end of the dormitory. The boy that is here with burns says [the] others went in with him to get their clothes and he was the only one to get out again. No one thought of any one going back in. It was all so sudden. Everybody has been very kind to us....The Indian agent at Fort Lapwai came out to offer his services and then sent twenty-four cots and mattresses, 100 woolen blankets and boxes of underwear also some army uniforms to be made over." [8] Once again, the community rallied to help, and in the midst of their sorrow the sisters were able to rebuild and continue the work of the school.

Although the Slickpoo and Lewiston St. Joseph communities had been separately founded and incorporated, the sisters soon began to share ministries in the area. They took charge of St. Stanislaus School in Lewiston and continued to conduct the Indian school at Slickpoo. Some sisters began training to be nurses at St. Joseph's Hospital. The communities began to move together. With such a small and young group of sisters, there was always a question of

St. Stanislaus Church, standing between St. Joseph's Hospital and St. Stanislaus School, Lewiston

affiliation with a larger group. As early as 1906, Fr. Cataldo had written to Mother Agnes Gonzaga Ryan at Carondelet describing the situation of "these two institutions and these 20 novices," and asking for affiliation.[9] Although he did not get a positive response at that time, Cataldo must have held on to his dream.

From 1906 to 1912, the sisters in Idaho were placed under the direction of the Sisters of St. Joseph of Tipton who had continued to support the Idaho community in any way they could, sending them additional sisters when they were able. In 1910, with increasing vocations, the novitiate was moved from Slickpoo to Lewiston. By 1912, Mother Gertrude, superior of the Tipton community, decided it was time for a decision on affiliation with her community. Probably expecting that the bishop of Boise would support the proposal for affiliation, she came to Lewiston to meet with the sisters and Bishop Glorieux. The bishop surprised her by calling for a vote from the sisters. The vote was against affiliation, so he immediately held an election to determine the next superior of the group. Mother Angelica Heenan was elected superior general, and each sister was allowed to decide between belonging to the new Idaho community or the Tipton group. A few sisters elected to return to Tipton with Mother Gertrude. The others settled gratefully into their new identity as Sisters of St. Joseph of Idaho under the leadership of their well-loved Mother Angelica.

About this time Pasco, another small frontier town over a hundred miles to the west, was developing, sharing an historical distinction with Lewiston—both areas had witnessed the passage of the Lewis and Clark expedition in the early 1800's. Pasco had its beginnings in 1879 when the Northern Pacific Railroad pushed its tracks south and west to the confluence of the Snake and

Mother Angelica Heenan, beloved general superior of the Sisters of St. Joseph of Idaho

Columbia Rivers to create a center for railroad and shipping transportation. Pasco was officially incorporated on September 3, 1891 and, along with the little town of Kennewick across the river, began to experience slow and steady growth.

As the little towns grew, they began to experience the need for medical services. Dr. H.B. O'Brien, who came to Pasco in 1908 along with a few other doctors, described the town's first effort at a public hospital—a three-bed hospital set up in an old residence about 1910. "'The doctors did their operating in the kitchen and used the wash boiler for a sterilizer.' It wasn't too satisfactory an arrangement, but it was better than nothing." [10]

In May 1915, a new pastor arrived at St. Patrick's Catholic parish in Pasco. Father W.B. Bender, a visionary and energetic leader, saw the need not only for a hospital but also for religious instruction for the children in the parish. Knowing that a parochial school was out of the question, he wrote to several groups of women religious asking for sisters to open a small hospital in Pasco and to provide education in Christian doctrine. "The first groups Father Bender approached turned him down, but he was persistent and he had the substantial elements of the community behind him. A friend finally aided him in putting the problem before Mother Borgia, sister superior of the hospital operated in Lewiston, Idaho, by the Sisters of St. Joseph." [11] Mother Borgia was finally able to promise sisters and, with the approval of the bishops of Boise and Spokane dioceses, six sisters of St. Joseph made the journey from Lewiston to Pasco, arriving on September 8, 1916.

Things moved very quickly then. Under the leadership of Mother Augustine Linnegar, the sisters leased the small two-story Montana Hotel on South 5th Street from Mrs. Anna Crotty, one of the first Catholics to settle in Pasco. With very few resources but with deep faith in God and a great desire to care for the sick of the community, dedicated physicians and community members helped the sisters make the dream a reality. Area businesses helped furnish the patient rooms, a community drive raised $800, and local physicians donated $500 worth of surgical and sterilizing equipment from their own offices. In the sixteen days after their arrival in Pasco, helped by hard-working Pasco housewives, the sisters scrubbed the hotel, set up

The Montana Hotel, site of Pasco's first hospital, 1916

beds, gathered meager equipment and furnishings, and prepared for the opening of Our Lady of Lourdes Hospital on September 24, 1916.

During the first year, the hospital admitted 607 patients. "The old hotel building hadn't been intended for a hospital. There were no elevators, of course, and the stairs were narrow and crooked. Getting a patient possibly suffering from post-operative shock out of the surgery and downstairs to the room was tricky business, requiring careful manipulation of the stretcher which couldn't be held level around corners on the stairs which barely permitted a passage."[12] The sisters were known to go out on the street to ask strong men to help carry patients down that staircase.

The Montana Hotel had served as a hospital for Pasco for only two years when the 1918 flu epidemic put incredible pressures on the tiny hospital. Cots filled every available space, the nursing staff worked impossible hours. Doctors gave up their office calls and tried to care for patients in their homes whenever possible, getting their sleep in their automobiles while being driven from one call to the next. Clearly, a new and larger hospital was needed.

By this time, Mother Borgia, an able hospital administrator, had replaced Mother Augustine at Lourdes. She worked with a hospital committee and community leaders to raise funds and find a suitable location, negotiating with the Northern Pacific Railway to buy an entire block on Fourth Street adjacent to St. Patrick's Church for the sum of $1.00. Construction began for the 50-bed hospital in July 1920. The original estimate for the building was $80,000, but because of construction difficulties, the final cost when the building opened on July 29, 1921 was $140.000.

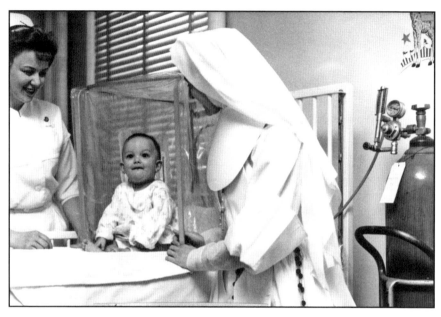

Sr. Teresa Marie McIntier, Our Lady of Lourdes

As the sisters struggled with debt, help came from an unexpected source. A Jesuit priest, Fr. Edward J. Brown, joined the hospital as its first chaplain bringing not only his pastoral gifts but also his sound financial skills. He sent out countless letters collecting thousands of dollars of bad debts. Payments were not always in cash, but the sisters could usually make use of farm products offered in lieu of cash. Fr. Brown brought many blessings to Lourdes during his few years as chaplain. At his death in 1925, a doctor remarked that his name would be mentioned for generations to come by the many friends who loved him so dearly.

Sr. de Chantal, who was missioned as a young sister to Lourdes in 1919, enjoyed reminiscing about those early days. She remembered cold mornings when she served coffee to the sisters after they gathered in the warm kitchen for morning prayer and the litany of the Sacred Heart. She recalled that the new hospital stood in open fields and when the wind blew, clouds of dust and sand rose sky high. The sisters would run out after a wind storm to brush off window sills on the ground floor before opening windows for the day. Landscaping began with a few catalpa and cottonwood trees, then a grassy lawn, until finally the sisters were able to plant flower beds.[13]

The terrible flu of 1918 was more devastating for the Lewiston hospital than for Lourdes. Sr. Mary Evangelista Wark was the first of the sisters to die in October 1918. At one time, fourteen nursing and

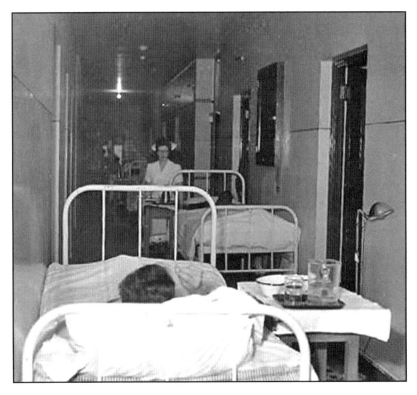

Over-crowded at Our Lady of Lourdes Hospital

teaching sisters were all sick at once. Out at the mission, school was closed and as many children as possible were sent to their homes. This allowed a few Slickpoo sisters to come into Lewiston and help out at the hospital.

In a November 26, 1918 letter, Sr. Aloysius described the scene at the hospital. "Mr. Mann and his wife and two babies are here. They are very sick. The babies are down in the Sisters' community room most of the time. Mother Angelica looks bad….Sr. Clement died yesterday. Mother (Angelica) does not know she is dead and we do not intend to tell her. I was with Sr. Evangelista (Wark) when she died and was her undertaker. They brought the casket up on the back porch….They gave me a sheet soaked in bichloride and I wrapped it around Sister. She did not have her linens on or her rosary. When I was alone I opened the casket and dressed Sister with her veil and rosary and guimpe. I want when I die to have every piece of my holy habit on….The halls are filled with beds and sick; three came in the last night. One died at 12 midnight; the next one went in the same bed and died at 4:00 a.m…..We count each other every morning." [14]

When it was over, eight sisters of St. Joseph had died in twenty months, including their General Superior, Mother Angelica Heenan. It was a shocking loss to the little band of sisters and to the town of Lewiston. Tribute was paid to Mother Angelica in the *Lewiston Morning Tribune*: "She was a valiant woman, free of bravado, a perfect lady in delicacy of feeling and culture of manner. Her charity to the sick and suffering was only surpassed by her tenderness and compassion toward the Indian children and orphans. She had the power to uplift the drooping spirit and inspire the despondent. Her justice was tempered with true charity and prudence." [15]

Added to the losses of so many sisters, the community was also struggling with financial problems associated with expanding the Lewiston hospital, opening the hospital in Pasco, and maintaining the Indian school and two recently opened nursing schools. Mother Borgia, who came back to Lewiston from Pasco to become General Superior in 1922, recognized that the little group could not survive on its own much longer. She had visited St. Louis in 1916 exploring the idea of affiliation with the Sisters of St. Joseph of Carondelet, but at that time the Lewiston sisters had not supported the idea. On July 29, 1924, she wrote Carondelet again. "I have prayed ever since to have our community united to the original foundation and now I think nearly all the older sisters would consent and with the approval of our Right Reverend Bishop I again wish to apply for affiliation. We number 50 sisters and 4 novices....I wish that you could come to see us and decide in our favor." Two months later, she wrote again thanking Mother Agnes Rossiter for the affirmative decision. "My councilors and nearly all of the sisters want to be affiliated, and will be very glad to be subject to a Mother Provincial. That is why I am applying to have a mother to go to."[16] When the Idaho sisters voted on affiliation in October, there were only two dissenting votes.

After visiting the Idaho sisters in March 1925, Mother Agnes Rossiter wrote to the Bishop in Boise: "We were most favorably impressed by our visit to the Northwest, and by the great work that has been accomplished there for God and souls. There is a wonderful future for the Church in your beautiful state, and I consider it a privilege to cooperate with you, through our dear Sisters in Lewiston, in the development of that future."[17] Meanwhile, the Idaho sisters, given the choice of belonging to the St. Paul or the Los Angeles province, decided in favor of Los Angeles.

The procedures for affiliation took a year to complete with communications slow and approvals even slower in Rome. Reverend Mother Agnes Rossiter wrote to Mother Borgia in August 1925: "All we have to do now is to await the decree, which will most likely be here soon, though a 'little time' in Rome seems a long time to us, accustomed as we are to doing things up so quickly. However, we know that Rome's approval is assured."[18]

By November 1925, twenty-one years after Father Cataldo's arrival with the twelve young women from Philadelphia, all approvals were complete. Mother Mary Margaret Brady, Provincial Superior of the Los Angeles Province, came to the Northwest with Mother Agnes Rossiter to receive the fifty-two Idaho sisters and one novice formally into the congregation. Simple ceremonies were held during Mass in Lewiston, Slickpoo, and Pasco. Mother Agnes wrote later to the Bishop: "The sisters, without exception, were happy to see us and to fulfil every condition necessary to transform them from Sisters of St.

Joseph of Lewiston to Sisters of St. Joseph of Carondelet. We met with the same enthusiastic reception at Slickpoo and Pasco as at Lewiston, and left all the sisters very happy and contented. Their dispositions are admirable, and such as must draw down God's blessing on the affiliation so successfully brought about." [19]

As integration into the larger congregation slowly proceeded, not all went smoothly. There were new customs to learn, new ways of living community, different prayer styles. The Lewiston novitiate was closed and novices sent to the novitiate at St. Mary's Academy in Los Angeles. Above all, a trust level needed to be built with their first superior who had been assigned to them from the St. Paul province. Gradually, though, as the Idaho sisters began to be more comfortable with being part of the western province, their ministries grew and vocations continued to flourish. The hope of Mother Agnes began to be fulfilled that God's blessing would be drawn down on the affiliation so successfully brought about.

The mission school at Slickpoo, Fr. Cataldo's original dream, was always a financial struggle. The mission had never received funds from the United States Department of Indian Affairs, although the Drexel Foundation had sent money often. The sisters needed to continue a regular routine of begging for many years to keep the mission functioning. As time went on, the character of the mission continued to change. The bishop of Boise consolidated all the orphanages of the diocese at Culdesac where the Slickpoo mission was located, and the mission was renamed St. Joseph's Orphanage. Eventually parish and government charities began to offer help, and maintaining the home became a little easier.

By 1968, changes in the foster care system and the development of government systems of child care led the community and the Bishop to make the decision to close St. Joseph's Orphanage. The site of the mission school, not far from Fr. Cataldo's original St. Joseph Mission Church, is still visited by Sisters of St. Joseph who treasure the opportunity the community had to be part of the mission to the Indians in the Northwest.

CHAPTER 6

BUILDING THE MOUNT

"Sisters, this is the place to choose. It gives promise of great development by which a college should be surrounded."

Reverend Mother Mary Agnes Rossiter

Two months before the Idaho community became part of the western province of the Sisters of St. Joseph, Mount St. Mary's College enrolled its charter class in Los Angeles. As Provincial Superior, Mother Mary Margaret Brady had played an active role in the process of the Idaho affiliation and, with Reverend Mother Agnes Rossiter, officiated at the formal ceremonies in November. Meanwhile, back home in Los Angeles, an absorbing part of her work in the preceding two years had been the idea of establishing a four-year Catholic college for women.

Sr. Dolorosa Mannix, one of the founders of the college, describes how Bishop John Cantwell jump-started the thinking. "The inception of the idea which resulted in the founding of Mount St. Mary's College dated from 1923, following the commencement exercises at St. Mary's Academy. [The Bishop], impressed by the large number of charming girls in the graduating class, earnestly requested ...Mother Margaret Mary Brady to consider the establishment of a college at the earliest possible opportunity."[1]

With the explosion of Los Angeles population in the 1920s and the corresponding demand for Catholic schools, the time was ripe for development of Catholic higher education. The Jesuits' Loyola College of Los Angeles developed from St. Vincent's College for Boys which had closed in 1911. Incorporated in 1918, the college grew rapidly and moved from the downtown location to the Westchester campus in 1929, achieving university status in 1930. Immaculate Heart College in Hollywood began as a secondary school in 1906 and became a college in 1916. When Bishop Cantwell appealed to the initiative of the Sisters of St. Joseph, what he dreamed of was another four-year Catholic college for women.

Mother Margaret Mary was used to leadership. She had been superior at the Academy of Our Lady of Peace, directress at St. Mary's Academy, assistant provincial superior with Mother Marcella Manifold, general councilor to Mother Agnes Rossiter, and in 1923 was just beginning two terms as Provincial Superior in Los Angeles. She saw the importance of a college as a ministry of the province to offer young women an opportunity to receive a liberal education in a Christian environment. In addition, in letters to Reverend Mother Agnes Rossiter, she pointed out that as the number of sisters increased, they could be educated more easily and at far less expense in a college owned and staffed by the congregation.[2]

With the encouragement of Bishop Cantwell and the approval of the General Council, plans came together and the college was incorporated under the name of Mount St. Mary's College, receiving its charter on October 15, 1925, the date also celebrated as the founding of the Sisters of St. Joseph. "Thus," commented Sr. Dolorosa in her reminiscences, "by a happy coincidence, Founders Day falls on the birthday of our Community." In his remarks at the dedication of the college on October 17, 1925, the bishop said, "The inauguration of a collegiate department is the realization of the fondest hopes of the sisters who desired to place a capital stone upon the many educational structures that they so efficiently preside over in the diocese."[3]

Mother Margaret Mary was named the first president of the college, a position she held until 1937. Five Sisters of St. Joseph comprised the full-time faculty: Sisters Agnes Bernard Cavanaugh, history; Mary Dolorosa Mannix, Latin and English; Celestine Quinn, music; M. Winifred Riecker, vocal; and Mary Ignatia Cordis, art. Four part-time teachers taught religion, philosophy, English, physics, and French.

A story, perhaps apocryphal, describes the first efforts of

recruitment. Early in the summer of 1925, the sisters proposed to the Academy's graduating class that they become the charter members of Mount St. Mary's College. The class of 1925 caught the spirit and became the nucleus of the first freshman class. The college registered its first students, twenty-five in number, in September l925, squeezed into available space at St. Mary's Academy. Classes were held in the novitiate classroom, and science laboratories were shared with the high school.

Of these charter members, ten persevered through the four years, receiving their degrees in June 1929. Mrs. Lillian May Evans, speaking of these early years, said recently, "That first year of college was the happiest school experience of my life. We had that one little room only, but we had excellent teachers and a close sympathetic contact with them which formed lasting friendships." The charter class set out to establish structure and traditions, drawing up the first constitutions for student government and designing a uniform for the student body—white blouse with tan tweed skirt and jacket.

Enrollment grew rapidly at the new college, as well as the academy, and the sisters began planning for expansion. "In the spring of 1926, plans were formulated for the erection of an additional building on the academy grounds. Happily Mother Margaret had saved for a building fund." The new building called College Hall included four classrooms, a library on the first floor and sleeping quarters on the second floor for the fifteen resident students.

Soon Mother Margaret Mary and her councilors began to look for property for the future site of the college. After visiting every section of the city, they settled on a tract in the foothills of the Santa Monica Mountains. Sr. Dolorosa, by then dean of the college, was in the group that first visited the site. The property was "at the confluence of two roads running through what was then called Boehme Canyon....When the real estate agents took us to the site, there was no road, and the climb had to be made through the brush, mostly sage, chaparral, and sumac. The guide sent his dog ahead of us saying, 'If there is a rattlesnake in the brush, the dog will bark.' We were grateful that the dog did not bark, though we did see rattlers coiled around the branches of the black walnut on the summit....The new site was a promontory, eleven hundred feet above sea level overlooking Los Angeles, and six coast towns. A view of forty miles of ocean stretching from the Santa Barbara Channel Islands to the Catalinas and Palos Verdes hills on the west, and on the east an inspiring view of mountain ridges, one, Mount Baldy, being snow-capped most of the year."

Reverend Mother Agnes Rossiter, visiting the province at the time, made the climb up through the brush and gave her unqualified approval, mentioning the beauty of the location and the proximity to the state university in the neighborhood. [4] "Sisters, this is the place to choose. It gives promise of great development by which a college should be surrounded." [5]

Traditional histories of the college agree that the thirty-six acre site was purchased in 1928 at $4500 an acre from the Rodeo Land and Water Company of Los Angeles. But recent research into college archives has revealed a totally different story. The only grant deed in the files shows that the sisters paid a total of ten dollars to the Los Angeles Mountain Park Company in 1929 for a total of 33 1/3 acres. How to explain that college records show only the one traditional story, and yet the sale filed with Los Angeles County tells another? Victoria McCargar, archivist for Mount St. Mary's College, wrote in the college magazine giving some insights into land sales in that Los Angeles boom period, but no final explanation.

Sr. Dolorosa told how the final twenty acres were added to the property. "Mother Margaret Mary was anxious to buy an additional twenty acres which overlooked the college on the north. The price, however, of $90,000 made this impossible." Ten years later, however, Mother Marie de Lourdes, then president, was able to secure it for $10,000, bringing the college campus to about 55 acres.

Planning progressed rapidly. "The first building was designed to follow the contour of the hill, ranging from one to five stories. This was to be called the Faculty Building, the present Brady Residence Hall." This building, designed with Spanish Gothic concrete and tiled architecture, housed the entire college for a few years—classrooms, laboratories, library, kitchen, dining rooms, laundries, private rooms or sleeping porches for students, prefects and faculty, a lounge and small chapel. "The contractor, John F. Brennan, not

From the Archives

According to the "official" history, Mount St. Mary's College paid $4,500 an acre to the Rodeo Land & Water Co. for the 33 1/3 acres that became the Chalon Campus. Although $150,000 was a lot of money in 1929, today it seems like a spectacular bargain.

The "real" story, however, is even better. According to a recently discovered grant deed, the sisters paid the Los Angeles Mountain Park Co. a grand total of $10 for the property. Talk about bargains.

Real estate developers in the 1920s knew that a college campus could anchor a new neighborhood and boost sales. A number of similar deals date from that time, including a donation of land for UCLA. Foremost among donors was oilman Alphonzo Bell. His companies, including the Los Angeles Mountain Park Co., developed the mountain front from Sepulveda Boulevard to the ocean. Bell contributed part of the UCLA campus and even tried to persuade his alma mater, Occidental College, to relocate to the Westside. As generous as he was, the area of Brentwood Heights that became the Mount also fit nicely into his sales strategy.

So where did the discrepancy in Mount history come from? That remains a mystery. The Rodeo Land & Water deal is written into the College's corporate minutes of March 25, 1929. The grant deed with Los Angeles Mountain Park was recorded with Los Angeles County six months later, on Sept. 29, 1929. The later deal was never recorded in the minutes.

Was it oversight or error, or did something suddenly change? Maybe someday the facts will emerge. In the meantime, the "real" history is every bit as interesting as the "official" one.

Victoria McCargar, college archivist [6]

---

too happy over difficulties in the way of getting his building supplies in place, commented, 'The sisters have certainly bought a view.'"

As the new campus developed, the academic structure of the college was being solidified. Negotiations with the state began in summer 1928 for approval of courses leading to California teaching credentials, and an affiliation with UCLA's education department was established so university professors could become members of the Mount education staff. Dean Marvin L. Darsie, chair of UCLA's education department, became head of the Mount's education department until his death in 1940. In addition to offering courses, he worked with the assistant to the State Superintendent of Education to advise the Mount in selecting courses for the elementary and secondary credentials.

Brady Hall construction, Mount St. Mary's College

In 1928, the Mount initiated programs for nurses, either registered or those in training, offering a one-year course as preparation for nursing training, and a two-year course for registered nurses leading to the B.S. degree. St. Vincent's Hospital was an early part of this program, followed by St. Joseph's Hospital in Orange, Mercy Hospital in San Diego, St. Luke's in Altadena, St. Mary's in Tucson, and St. Francis in Honolulu.[7]

Involving the students in service projects was an early part of the curriculum. St. Joseph's Guild was introduced in 1927 with the assistance of Rev. R. E. Lucey of the diocesan Catholic welfare program. Devoted to social service, Guild members offered assistance to the needy such as sewing, collecting funds, securing teachers for the Diocesan Confraternity of Christian Doctrine, and giving occasional entertainments for the Mexican settlement centers. The establishment of a department of sociology soon followed, designed to prepare students for master's work in social welfare.[8]

Music was always an important department. The Bishop Cantwell School of Liturgical Music was inaugurated as a Mount department in 1931 with the purpose of cooperating with the Bishop in the work of reform of church music as decreed in the 1903 encyclical *Motu Proprio* of Pope Pius X. "The liturgical choir of the school, consisting of seventy-five women, made its initial appearance in a program of Gregorian chant at [UCLA's] Royce Hall on May 8, 1931."[9] In 1929,

Sr. Celestine's orchestrated symphonic poem from Francis Thompson's *Hound of Heaven* was included in a University of Southern California concert presenting compositions of contemporary artists. Sr. Celestine later received the degree of Doctor of Music from the university and headed the Mount's music department for many years.

In 1929, the Mount met the standards to be recognized by the Northwestern Association, the only standardizing agency on the west coast at that time. By 1930, the college was affiliated with the Catholic University of America and recognized by the Association of American Colleges. The next year, the Mount was a charter member of the new Association of Colleges and Universities of the Pacific Southwest which eventually became the standardizing agency for California colleges.

On June 16, 1929, four years after the founding of the college, Mount St. Mary's conferred its first degrees. Sr. Dolorosa described it: "This feature formed part of the ground-breaking ceremonies on the new college site. For the occasion a platform was erected and decorated with bunting, with seating for the guests of honor. On a sloping hillside nearby, the seats were provided for an orchestra and student body—a unique and attractive setting. Untrue to California weather and so unexpected, it poured rain the night before, leaving a cold day and bedraggled decorations. The program went forward as scheduled." Eight graduates received the Bachelor of Arts degree, and two the Bachelor of Music.

Present on that bedraggled platform were notables of the city of Los Angeles: Bishop Cantwell; Dr. Rufus von Kleinsmid, President of the University of Southern California; Reverend Joseph Sullivan, S.J., President of Loyola University; Isidore B. Dockweiler, prominent Los Angeles lawyer and politician; John Steven McGroarty, poet laureate of California; Paul McCormick, federal judge on the United States District Court; novelist Frank Hamilton Spearman; and other friends and civic officials. About 2000 guests attended the graduation, traveling to the hilltop on the unpaved Chalon Road which gave access to the campus from Sepulveda Boulevard. Bundy Drive had not yet been constructed.[10]

By February 1931, some classes were held in the almost-finished new building, but the official move of the college to the new campus did not happen until April 12, Easter Sunday. The Academy's little blue bus, driven by Marceline Mamake, the Academy's driver, arrived loaded with boxes of books and notebooks, sisters' baggage, bedding, and eight sisters of St. Joseph. Sr. Dolorosa recollected "that a pillow was sticking out the window and a mattress had been hastily stuffed in, in case of emergency. Trucks loaded with furniture, barrels of dishes, trunks, and other necessaries had been going up during the past week, but our bus was carrying the last minute pick ups….As classes were to open the following day, and some of our thirteen resident students were returning from their Easter vacation that night, we and the dishes had to be there to receive them.

"We drove up Bundy Drive into Boehme Canyon…up to the abrupt turn at the valley end of an unpaved Chalon Road, which bulldozers had cut out of the mountain….The road terminated at the top level, where stood the residence hall alone, facing two unplanted terraces and wide cleared area, its mountain top lopped off, strewn with shale and uncleared plaster from the building."

"That evening saw a small group of sisters weary from unpacking dishes, carrying beds, and necessary chores….Safe, as we thought, in the privacy of the kitchen ten hundred feet above the valley, [we] stood or sat if one could find a chair, about the dish washer table….Looking toward the windows we were startled to see at each pane a curious face pressed against the glass. The nearest neighbors from a distance of two to four miles had been led by curiosity to see what was going on in 'the college upon the hill.' They were invited to return for a daylight visit and tour of inspection."

With the arrival of the students on April 13, the new campus was filled with life and activity. Those founding sisters played multiple roles. They would teach their classes or staff the dean's or registrar's offices, then rush off in late afternoon to peel potatoes in the kitchen, eat a hasty dinner, do all the dishes from the students' dining room, then walk outside to enjoy the cool of the evening. They would watch for car lights coming up Bundy. Since neighbors were few, a car coming up the road was almost certain to be someone they knew, or perhaps a new student coming to enroll. Those first sisters reminisced about the warm nights with the smell of lemon and orange blossoms floating up from the valley to delight them. They

Pioneers of the Mount. Seated from left Sr. Generosa Wall, Mother Margaret Brady, Sisters Dolorosa Mannix, Celestine Quinn. Standing from left Sisters Gertrude Joseph Cook, Rose de Lima Lynch, Ursula Flynn, Rosemary Lyons, Ignatia Cordis.

also had a clear memory of waking up one morning in May, about a month after they had moved the college to the mountain top, to four inches of snow on the ground. Classes were delayed that day after the arrival of the bus with the commuting students so they could play in the snow.[11]

By the time the college was established on the new campus, the country was deep into the Great Depression. Just four months after the Chalon groundbreaking and first graduation, the stock market crashed with severe effects on every level of the economy of America and the world. And on the college. The sisters struggled and prayed along with the rest of the nation as they continued construction of the new building, hired staff for development and maintenance of the property, and probably counted every penny as they planned future growth. A significant addition to the staff in 1932 was Martin Bullinger, a much-loved figure on campus who served for decades as chief engineer and campus superintendent. Improvement of access roads led to the development of the Bowl in 1935, a terraced amphitheatre which provided a site for graduations until 1953. During the darkest days of the Depression, the sisters continued to nurture the building fund for the college chapel. Their dream of a

Mary Chapel, Chalon Campus

chapel crowning the mountain became a reality in 1939 with a Christmas Midnight Mass in Mary Chapel. Going up at the same time was the faculty residence hall, completed during the summer of 1940.[12]

During the war years, courses focused on topics like international relations, understanding of the world situation, and preparation for a just peace. First Aid and Home Nursing were added to the curriculum with more than three-fourths of the student body enrolled. Students became active in volunteer work, sale of war bonds, sponsorship of blood donation on campus, and preparation for possible air attacks. Fire squads were formed to handle incendiary bombs and residence buildings equipped with sand stations and blackout curtains. Nightly dimming of college lights was always a problem, with sixty forgetful resident students.[13] Sister Dolorosa reminisced, "Some of the neighbors became hysterical and one woman phoned, 'I just love your chapel, but would you mind painting it black?' Another less friendly, yet hysterical gentleman said, 'Your chapel tower sticks up like a sore thumb.' Another female called up, 'We shall notify the police if you do not keep your lights turned out.'"[14]

Plans to add a fourth building to the campus had to be put on hold during the war because of scarcity of steel and other building materials needed for the war effort. But in the 1943-44 academic year, enrollment in science courses increased so significantly that the college requested priority status for the building project. "The need for trained women technicians and chemists caused the federal government to put Mount St. Mary's College on the building-priority list, so the building permit was granted."[15]

St. Joseph's Hall opened for classes in the 1945 fall term with fully equipped science laboratories, classrooms, administrative offices, home economics facilities, and a little theater. Another major addition to the college campus was the Charles Willard Coe Memorial Library, dedicated in 1947.

The Mount's strong tradition of scientific research began in the 1940s with collaboration in cancer research with Dr. Joseph A. Pollia, director of the Frank H. Boyer Foundation for cancer research. After Dr. Pollia's death in 1951, Sr. Gertrude Joseph Cook continued the project at UCLA Medical School for another decade. Joining the biological sciences department in 1947, Sr. Mary Gerald Leahy began a career of research that brought her a worldwide reputation. Following in these footsteps, the department developed an outstanding research-based curriculum emphasizing student collaboration in the active research programs of the faculty.

Sr. Mary Gerald Leahy

Sr. Mary Gerald Leahy was a fascinating mix of progressive, creative sister and a world renowned research biologist. Born and raised in San Francisco, she entered the Sisters of St. Joseph in 1936. Her first mission was teaching elementary school. She loved it and probably expected to teach little children all her life, but after four years, to her regret, she was sent to the University of Southern California for undergraduate study and the Catholic University of America for a masters degree in biology. God was leading her into another world—college teaching and research.

After some years teaching at Mount St. Mary's College, she went on to complete her doctorate at Notre Dame University. In a personal essay, she described how it was strongly

(continued on next page)

impressed on the doctoral students that they would have a responsibility to continue research for the sake of Catholic higher education, science, and life "So I incorporated into my teaching a Special Problems course which allowed students to participate in my research." Her research, funded by the National Institutes of Health, the World Health Organization, and the National Science Foundation, was focused on insect reproductive physiology.

In her years in the Mount's biology department from the 1940s to the 1980s she was loved and respected for many things, but best known for her mosquitos—properly tagged, and usually kept safe in her laboratory. Her reputation reached far beyond California, however, for its medical and economic importance. Countries all over the world sought her insights in controlling insect-carried diseases like malaria, yellow fever, and hemorrhagic fever. In 1966, she was at Harvard on a postdoctoral fellowship and stayed on for another year as an NIH visiting scientist. The next year she was in Israel to study the accessory glands of ticks, tick pheromones and reproduction. Requests for consultation and public lectures took her to Scotland, Australia, Bangkok, Teipei, Japan, Honolulu, Nigeria and Kenya ("Kenya was my favorite").

Gerald brought along her faith and identity as a sister of St. Joseph on her travels. "My associates were usually scientists who had never worked with a nun. After we became friends they would often ask more searching questions about God and life than did college students at home. These have been wonderful learning experiences and I feel like I've left a part of my heart with my friends in each part of the world."

Sr. Gerald was in Czechoslovakia in 1979 when she suffered a stroke. After hospitalization, she was able to complete the five months of her stay. But as her health diminished, she saw it as a change in God's plan for her. "The experience of my stroke challenged my spiritual and psychological resources. But I now know it as a caressing stroke of God for out of it has come a deeper consciousness of Life." She came home, received training in clinical pastoral education, and began ministry as a hospital chaplain. By now, she had changed her religious name to her baptismal name of Mary.

Mary Leahy's reading and experience were wide-ranging, her friendships vast and varied. In a Christmas letter a few years before her death in 2004, she expressed her love for family and friends in the language of her personal world view: "In many aspects our relationship has continued to grow: for that I am grateful. We are each ever-differentiating spokes of energy from the same source, yet differences enrich and support us."

Instructions left for her funeral mentioned readings from Teilhard de Chardin, Jung, Gerard Manley Hopkins ("The world is charged with the grandeur of God"), Rabindranath Tagore, and Brian Swimme ("invite him to the Mass!"). As one of the readings for the funeral Mass, she requested Ephesians 3:20-21, a passage that must have expressed her probing searches into the inner and external worlds of God. In her words—"God is more powerful than you can imagine."

The 1950s saw the celebration of the 25th anniversary of the Mount's founding and the inauguration of a nursing program, offering the first Bachelor of Science in Nursing in the state. Initiated and nurtured by Sr. Rebecca Doan, nursing became one of the strongest elements of the college curriculum. Two more buildings went up in the fifties—Marian Hall of Fine Arts in 1956 and Carondelet Hall, the second residence hall, in 1959. Meanwhile, major construction was going on in the lowest tip of Mount property for the new provincialate and novitiate of the Sisters of St. Joseph. The 1955 move to the House of Studies from St. Mary's Academy positioned a new center for the province and brought many young sister students to the college.

Another generation of Mount sisters. From left Sisters Laurentia Digges, Catherine Therese Knoop, Germaine McNeil, Rose Gertrude Calloway, Catherine Anita Fitzgerald, Patricia Zins, Aline Marie Gerber, Ignatia Cordis.

When Sr. Rebecca Doan became the Mount's seventh president in fall 1961, she was quickly confronted with a natural disaster—a devastating brush fire. In a college publication, Sr. Joseph Adele Edwards told the story. "While three minor brush fires had threatened the Mount in years past with little or no damage, this was not the case on Monday, November 6, 1961, at 8 a.m. On this second day of extreme heat and Santa Ana winds, accidental sparks ignited and started what became known as the Bel Air/Brentwood fire. It eventually burned 12,000 acres and destroyed 484 homes and 21 other structures, including...the Sisters' convent and Marian Hall. While flames roared up the east and west hillsides, both the House of Studies and the College were evacuated." Sisters, students, and faculty waited at evacuation locations off campus, watched the flames and smoke engulfing the mountain, and prayed. The fire was not fully contained until evening of the second day, but the campus had been declared safe for occupancy that morning. "A wise Sr. Rebecca knew that normalcy was the best policy and immediately led the clean-up brigade. Mount students, faculty, and staff welcomed the help brought by the navy crewmen of the U.S.S. Hornet and students and faculty from Loyola University."[16] Classes resumed at 8 a.m. Wednesday morning once broken glass had been swept off desk surfaces and with a cold wind blowing in the empty windows. The academic year was back on track.

Sr. Rebecca had her hands full with another major development in the college during her term. When she became president, a few Mount classes were already being offered at Chester Place, the Edward L. Doheny estate near downtown Los Angeles. Mrs. Carrie Estelle Doheny, the widow of the oil tycoon who died in 1935 and a major Los Angeles philanthropist, was a generous supporter of church and educational institutions. A friend of Mount St. Mary's College since its early days, she had offered the use of one of the homes on her property for classes in the summer of 1957.

The first teachers on the Doheny grounds were Sisters Regina Clare Salazar, Albert Mary Rebel, Monica Miller, and Colette McCann. Mrs. Doheny must have kept a benevolent eye on the academic activity next door to her mansion, sending over two huge bottles of purified water each week for the sisters who in turn kept an eye on the mansion, watching vegetable and flower delivery trucks driving up the sweeping approach every morning to the Doheny home.

College activity on the Doheny property increased in the next few years with the addition of late afternoon and evening classes for working adults unable to drive to the hilltop campus for their coursework. Then, on October 30, 1958, Mrs. Doheny died, leaving her extensive residential estate to the Archdiocese of Los Angeles. In the coming months and years, Cardinal McIntyre allowed the college to use a growing number of the mansions, and finally deeded the east side of Chester Place to Mount St. Mary's College provided it would always be used for educational purposes. Eventually, the entire Chester Place estate came into the possession of the college, first called the Downtown Campus, and finally the Doheny Campus.

In the fall of 1962, the Associate in Arts degree program was initiated at Doheny with 220 full-time students, making Mount St. Mary's the first Catholic college on the west coast to offer the A.A. degree. The location of the campus in the heart of the city encouraged the development of outstanding programs, including a center for urban education for inner-city teachers and administrators. The Cuban Teacher Training Institute began in 1965 as a grant-funded project to re-settle Cuban refugees as native Spanish-speaking teachers in the city's junior high schools.

Dr. Roman Young with three past presidents of Mount St. Mary's College. From left Sisters Cecilia Louise Moore, Magdalen Coughlin, Rebecca Doan.

When Edward L. Doheny and his wife bought their home in 1901, Chester Place was an elegant residential property of about 18 acres comprising 13 homes and extensive lawns and gardens. In time, the Dohenys purchased the entire complex and settled their friends in this exclusive residential park, grooming it into a showplace with their team of 17 gardeners. By the time the property came into college hands, it was an island of beauty and peace in a rapidly growing and diversifying downtown Los Angeles, bringing a priceless opportunity to the college to expand the range and depth of its offerings and bring them within reach of a much broader population. Advancing into the second half of the 20th century, the character of the college would be transformed.

The Mount's Doheny Campus

CHAPTER SEVEN

POST-WAR EXPLOSION OF GROWTH

"May God swamp you with vocations."

In August 1947, Mother Mary William Flanagan sat down to write a report to the congregational leadership on the state of the Los Angeles province. She had been provincial superior for the six years dominated by World War II. Her brief two-page report didn't waste words, listing province officers, location, census numbers, and province debt, and then describing the effects of wartime on the sisters.

"Food stamps were required for meat, butter, coffee, shoes, sugar and many other commodities. Gasoline was the sharpest. Troops were moved from one coast to the other. Priority was given to the service men on trains and buses. The diners were also open to the service men, and as a result, non-service people had to carry sufficient food for the trip from Portland to Los Angeles. Money was hard to get. Prices soared. The sisters made great sacrifices to help clear the [province] debt." Civil Defense required blackouts and training in first aid. The need to be alert to enemy attacks along the coast intensified worry about the sisters who had opened missions in Hawaii in 1938.

With the continuing expansion of the province,

Mother William Flanagan

money was always a challenge. "In a visit from Reverend Mother Pius in 1942, she suggested that we put up a building at the Mount to take care of administration offices and classrooms with laboratories for the sciences." Such a project must have seemed hopeless in wartime, but "we placed this project under the patronage of St. Joseph. Prayers were offered to St. Joseph each day in all the houses. Each week when the bill arrived for the expenses of the construction, there were always sufficient funds to meet the cost so that at the time of completion the debt on the building $345,000 was paid. Individual sisters made many sacrifices in prayer and financial help." The Mount's St. Joseph Hall was dedicated on March 25, 1945.

Mother William closed the report with the statement that the province debt of $813,000 had been cleared. "We attribute this great task to the sisters' devotion to St. Joseph." She added that despite the difficulties the province had experienced during those six years, "the sisters met the needs of the Church. This was made possible by the intercession of Divine Providence. The spiritual assets were very good as our prayer life deepened."

Census numbers included in Mother William's report show the increasing growth of the community. From 1941 to 1947, the total number of sisters in the province increased by 35, despite 27 deaths during those years. The number of postulants grew from 10 to 34, novices increased from 34 to 59. The steady increase in vocations was heartening, but not enough to meet the escalating requests for sisters' services. During her term, Mother William was able to mission sisters to only six new schools—two high schools in San Diego, three elementary schools in San Diego, Manhattan Beach, and Sonoma, and St. Joseph Home for Boys in Tucson. The situation was made more difficult in 1942 when Reverend Mother Pius recalled all the sisters from the St. Paul and St. Louis provinces who had been loaned to the west for some years. Mother William wrote that "this move made it difficult for the province to replace the sisters, as lay teachers were not acceptable at this time by pastors and parents."

The postwar years brought huge population growth to California. Military men and women had gotten a taste of the California climate and were migrating from all parts of the country. As newcomers settled in to raise their families, and as baby boomers began to come into school age, the pressure on the educational system became intense. Catholic parishes throughout the west expanded and multiplied, and struggled to meet the demand for quality Catholic education. As early as 1945, Mother William wrote to a pastor, "The mushroom growth of our schools and hospitals in the past few years has brought great stress and strain on the Province." Another pastor responded to a similar letter of refusal, "May God swamp you with vocations, so that I don't have to wait too long."

By the time Mother Rosemary Lyons became provincial in 1947, demands for sisters were coming from all parts of the country. Bishops and pastors, not yet open to the role of laity in Catholic education, flooded the provincialate with requests, not all of them calm. A priest wrote from South San Antonio, Texas, in 1949, "I am almost frantic. We shall have an 8-room school ready for September 1949. God was good. We got 3 surplus Government buildings enough for 8 classrooms and kindergarten and a sisters house. We need sisters. Can you possibly help us?....To date we have refusals from exactly 130 religious superioresses. Please help us for the love of God."

A year after Mother Rosemary became provincial, a new bishop came to Los Angeles. Archbishop James Francis McIntyre, soon to be named the first cardinal in the western United States, put his energy into planning for the enormous growth in the Catholic population. He located and purchased property all over southern California that would soon be used for parishes and schools. From 1948 to 1969, he opened 180 Catholic schools and 192 parishes. [1] As this explosion of growth continued, the Sisters of St. Joseph, along with other orders of men and women religious, responded to the limit of their resources.

In the years up to the mid-1940s, it had been rare that more than one new school or other ministry was opened each year by the sisters. In 1948, all that changed. That year, five schools were added. In the next 16 years, openings averaged from three to five a year, creating for the sisters a new El Camino Real stretching from San Diego and the southern coast to all areas of Los Angeles and the San Fernando Valley, the San Joaquin Valley, San Francisco and the East Bay, and east to Arizona. Finally in 1951, the King's Highway reached the

Pacific Northwest with the opening of St. Patrick's School in Pasco, Washington. Continuing the traditional commitment to secondary education, CSJs joined the staffs of religious men and women in a diocesan high school in Tucson, and in archdiocesan high schools in Torrance, Playa del Rey, and San Fernando.

These years of extraordinary growth sometimes called for heroic accomplishments. Sisters who entered the community in the early l940s tell of being sent out to a nearby school within days of putting on the postulant uniform to handle a primary grade. Sr. Anne Bernadette Stead recounts beginning teaching the Monday after she entered the convent at St. Mary's Academy. She was eighteen years old with one year of college. "We walked down the street from St. Mary's to St. John the Evangelist school" and began teaching that morning. She remembers that she had a time schedule and a lesson plan, but in her inexperience she had run through the whole day's plan by recess. A wiser teacher told her to start over, and this time to go deeper. The time schedule never left her hand all day. There weren't many people to ask for advice, so "we just did the best we could."

The CSJ supervisor for elementary schools came on weekends to help with planning and classroom methods. By the late l940s when multiple schools were opening with already stretched faculty, classrooms were overcrowded. New teachers frequently arrived on the first day to see sixty or more children in their desks, eyes on the door to see who their new teacher would be.

As new schools were opened, convents for the sisters were not always ready for them. Some sister teachers commuted to their schools from the Mount; more lived at St. Mary's Academy, leaving each morning in cars waiting for them, lined up in the sweeping circular drive at the Slauson entrance. The living situation was eased in 1948 when, in her unique way of controlling her environment, Mrs. Estelle Doheny purchased a residence on the back side of her property from a fraternity house of the University of Southern California and gave it to the Sisters of St. Joseph. Christened Infant of Prague Convent, this huge castle-like building on Figueroa Street became home for sisters ministering in inner city schools. It later served as a residence hall for Mount St. Mary's College, and finally—

The novitiate was full in the early 1950s.

renamed Stimson House—it returned to its former role as a CSJ residence.

During these years in the mid-century, as requests for new schools came from all parts of the western states and the works of the sisters multiplied, numbers of vocations grew as well. In 1941, Mother William had reported a total of 375 sisters. By 1951, the province had grown to 555; in 1961, the total was 870. In the late 1950s, novices numbered over 100.

Reception and profession ceremony in Carondelet Center chapel

There must have been days when the provincial superior felt a fulfillment of the prayer of the pastor begging God to swamp the community with vocations. In 1960, however, a steady decrease in vocations began and it continued even as the numbers of sisters in the province held firm. The total number of sisters in the Los Angeles province peaked at 894 in 1968, and then began a downturn. That year, there were only 21 novices in formation.

As overall numbers of sisters in the Los Angeles Province reached a plateau, 1965 was the last year for opening new missions on such a grand scale. Two elementary schools were opened this year in the San Francisco area—Most Precious Blood in Concord and Resurrection in Sunnyvale. And, under the leadership of Mother Josephine Feeley in this last year of her term as provincial superior, the province opened two CSJ-sponsored high schools for girls in Fresno and Concord, California.

The Sisters of St. Joseph had had a presence in the San Joaquin Valley since 1921 when St. Theresa School opened in Fresno. In the years following, they opened three more elementary schools in the valley—St. Joachim's in Madera and Our Lady of Victory and St. Anthony's in Fresno. And between 1935 and 1946, CSJs were assigned to St. Theresa's High School, a parochial secondary school serving a temporary need during the construction of San Joaquin Memorial, a central Fresno Catholic high school. Now in 1965, as the Catholic community in Fresno felt the need of a Catholic girls high school in the city, Monsignor James G. Dowling, Diocesan Superintendent of Schools and pastor of St. Theresa's, confidently turned to the Sisters of St. Joseph.

With plans for an eventual enrollment of 600-800 girls, construction began on Queen of the Valley Academy on a ten-acre site adjacent to St. Anthony's School. The academy, housed temporarily in one classroom and a small library room at St. Anthony's, opened on September 9, 1965, with a freshman class of 30 students. Sisters St. Joan Willert, principal, and Anne Eugene Metcalf opened the school, supported by a few lay faculty, and set about giving the new school its special character with uniforms, sports and sodality activities, and a choral program that first Christmas.

Moving day to the completed building on Friday, February 25, "found girls with books, folding desks, gym equipment and an accumulation of six months supply of assorted 'essentials' making the final trip across the empty field to the new school building. Photographers from two local TV stations as well as…from the Fresno Bee and the Central California Register were on hand for the historic move."[2] Classes began in the spacious new building on February 28, 1966.

Enrollment the first two years was healthy, with about 50 freshmen the second year and a larger number the third. But in the long run, enrollment turned around, becoming a serious problem. Nearby San Joaquin Memorial was increasingly attractive to students as a coed school with good extracurricular offerings and a strong sports program, as well as an attractive family tuition plan. In spite of the outstanding curriculum and quality of teaching at Queen of the Valley, families found they could not longer afford the higher tuition. After study of the situation, the decision had to be made to close Queen of the Valley. On June 2, 1973, with great regret, the Sisters of St. Joseph, the school and parish communities ended the eight-year history of the academy.

CSJ roots in the Oakland diocese go back to the previous century with the December 1883 opening of St. Joseph's Institute, later renamed St. Patrick's School. The colorful Fr. McNally, pastor of St. Patrick's parish, described his dream of the sisters coming to open his school as ready, able, active, energetic, zealous, and ardent in the fervor of God. That zeal and energy was poured into education and work with the deaf, and the ministry of the sisters in the San Francisco Bay area flourished and grew for over 80 years. By 1965, the sisters' schools dotted the landscape from San Jose north to San Francisco, Oakland, and out into the East Bay. And a secondary school was in the planning stages.

A few years earlier, in 1962, Bishop Floyd Begin, first bishop of Oakland, asked the Sisters of St. Joseph to found a girls' high school in the city of Concord. With the constant encouragement and financial assistance of the bishop, the sisters began to plan and design the school. Carondelet High School opened in September 1965 with only six classrooms available and construction ongoing.

Founding CSJs were Sisters Edward Mary Zerwekh, principal, Kathleen Kelly, Margaret Callahan, and two lay teachers.[3] The freshman class of 115 young women represented 25 feeder schools, many of them staffed by Sisters of St. Joseph.

A year later, the school was dedicated formally by Bishop Begin, Carondelet's close friend and supporter. With $2.1 million dollar construction completed on the spacious campus, the brick buildings, linked with graceful columns and balconies, suggested the Spanish-American heritage of California. As enrollment expanded, the school developed a solid reputation for excellence, innovation, and Christian community. By 1969, Carondelet had established a cooperative program with nearby De La Salle High School allowing juniors and seniors to attend selected classes on either campus, and setting up a common calendar and schedule, sharing of facilities, and joint faculty and student activities. The school continued to deepen its roots in Contra Costa County, eventually reaching its projected goal of 800 students.

Five former principals of Carondelet High School with their longtime secretary Kay Dietrich. From left Sisters Edward Mary Zerwekh, Kathleen Kelly, Barbara Cotton, Anne Eugene Metcalf, Kathleen Lang

One more high school was to be added to the list of CSJ-sponsored schools, but by a different path. When an archdiocesan high school opened in Lakewood, California in 1964, CSJs were invited to assume responsibility for its administration and staffing. Initially envisioned as co-ed in the pattern of other archdiocesan

St. Joseph's Day celebration at St. Joseph High School, Lakewood. Sitting from left Sisters Marianne Johnson, Margaret Jude Corey, Caroline Chang, Eileen Mary Connors. Standing from left Sisters Ann Patrick Plunkett, Dennis Anne Cremins, Jan Hsung, Janet Duffy, Pat Nelson, Myrtle Weyker.

schools, CSJs involved in the planning persuaded the archdiocesan decision-makers that an all-girls school was a greater need. Then they set about recruiting their first students in order to prove their point. A strong freshman enrollment was witness to parents' trust in "the sisters" to create a high school that would give their daughters an excellent education.

Sr. Mary Ursula Flynn served as the first principal with two other CSJs—Sisters Joan Louise Krause and Judith Lovchik—and a full complement of lay teachers when the school opened in 1964. These early CSJs, together with a dedicated staff of lay women and men, infused the CSJ mission and charism by their presence and ways of ministering. In 1990, the first lay principal, Dr. Terri Mendoza, energetically recruited CSJs to serve at St. Joseph's and worked tirelessly to sustain the CSJ spirit.

Although St. Joseph's was an archdiocesan school, it treasured its CSJ foundation and requested to be sponsored by the Sisters of St. Joseph. Recognizing the significance of the sponsorship relationship, province leadership approved St. Joseph's as a "philosophically" sponsored CSJ high school. This new designation signified an integral connection, but without the legal and canonical aspects of

St. Mary's Hospital, Tucson, 1955

traditional sponsorship. The school's commitment to "all that woman is capable of" and its CSJ spirit remain as essential aspects of its reputation for excellence.

While CSJs were opening schools all along the west coast, the work of the province's three hospitals was continually expanding. In Tucson, from its 12-bed origin in 1880, St. Mary's Hospital had grown to a capacity of 375 beds by the 1950s. Facing an acute hospital bed shortage with the rapid growth of Tucson's population in the mid-century, the sisters began a fund-raising campaign for a second hospital on the east side of the city. St. Joseph's Hospital was dedicated in 1961. In the 1980s, responding to the request of the Tucson diocese, the sisters took over management of a small Catholic hospital in Nogales, Arizona, eventually purchasing it, giving it the name of Carondelet Holy Cross Hospital.

In the Pacific Northwest, as the population in Lewiston and Pasco grew, St. Joseph's and Our Lady of Lourdes hospitals expanded services and added much needed facilities. In 1978, Mid-Columbia Mental Health, a facility serving the mentally ill in Richland, Washington, began to experience financial difficulties and sent a call for help to the three hospitals in the area. Only Lourdes responded, recognizing a perfect fit with the mission of the hospital, and Mid-Columbia merged with Lourdes Hospital. As Lourdes Counseling

Center, it is one of three psychiatric inpatient units in eastern Washington. In addition, it provides outpatient services to over 50% of publically funded mentally ill persons in southeastern Washington.

Although province healthcare ministry was thriving to the east and north, there was no CSJ hospital in California until the 1950s, but the idea of a Los Angeles hospital had been germinating since the mid-1930s when Sr. Rosaleen Lynch was principal of St. John Chrysostom School in Inglewood. The school was near the home of Grace Freeman Howland, daughter of Daniel Freeman, pioneer landowner and one of the founders of the city of Inglewood. Concerned about the safety of the children running out into the busy street from the school playground, St John's pastor suggested that Sr. Rosaleen ask Mrs. Howland to build a fence for the schoolyard. The fence was promptly built, and Mrs. Howland and the Sisters of St. Joseph began a long friendship.

Grace Freeman Howland cherished an idea of founding a hospital to honor the memory of her father. After discussions with the sisters, she deeded to the community nine acres of her property, then a wheat field, on Prairie and Grace Avenues where a general acute-care hospital would be built and

Plans for Daniel Freeman Hospital, Inglewood, October 1951. From left Mother Rosemary Lyons, actress Jeanne Crain, Mrs. Grace Freeman Howland, Sr. Rosaleen Lynch, George Ingland, mayor of Inglewood, Monsignor Thomas O'Dwyer, director of Catholic Charities and hospitals, and architect Al Martin, Jr. Photo by *Angeles Mesa News*.

named for her father. Fundraising began in 1950, administered by Sr. Mary Beatrice Johnson working with volunteer committee leaders from the local area. The entire South Bay was canvassed by volunteers going door-to-door asking for donations. Many came to the support of the sisters. "The first contribution, a $100 bond, came from one of the kitchen staff at Mount St. Mary's College. A boy in Inglewood sold Christmas cards and donated the money he raised. Several students from St. Eugene's School produced a musical show in a backyard theater and sold refreshments at intermission. Their $6.12 contribution bought a folding crib tray for the Pediatrics Department. The smallest contribution to the public campaign was 12 cents, the largest, $5,000. The doctors had their own goal of $100,000, and actually surpassed that figure." [4]

Groundbreaking in that nine-acre wheat field was held on November 2, 1952, and construction began the next month. During the following year, a new provincial superior came into office. One of the first tasks for Mother Rosaleen Lynch in her new leadership role was to oversee the final year of construction and planning for the hospital which had been made possible with her first meeting with her old friend Grace Freeman Howland. Sr. Anne Lucy Zieroff was appointed administrator for the hospital. The first staff included Sisters Mary Beatrice Johnson, Eleanore Francis Powers, Mary Stephen Maulsby, Monica Marie Knothe, and Julia Mary Farley. On Sunday, May 23, 1954, Daniel Freeman Memorial Hospital was dedicated by Cardinal McIntyre, and the doors opened the next day.

In the first eight weeks, the new hospital admitted 900 patients, and it was soon running at 100% occupancy. Already in 1956, a new wing was being planned to double the size of the hospital. In that same year, Mrs. Howland died and left to the sisters her 20-room home and an additional eleven acres with a generous bequest for hospital construction. Over the years, expansion continued and programs initiated to train x-ray and lab technicians. A groundbreaking program began in 1970 when Daniel Freeman became the birthplace of the paramedic system of emergency medicine for fire rescue squads and ambulance personnel.

Another program which brought national and international attention to Daniel Freeman was its outstanding rehabilitation

Daniel Freeman Hospital

diagnostic and treatment center. The hospital was designated by the federal government the official Comprehensive Rehabilitation Center for the western United States. In 1980, the Sisters of St. Joseph purchased a small struggling hospital in Marina del Rey, renaming it Daniel Freeman Marina Hospital. The acquisition of Marina brought the total beds in Daniel Freeman hospitals to 606.

Over the years, Daniel Freeman Memorial, together with St. Mary's Academy and St. John Chrysostom School across Grace Avenue, held a treasured position in the city of Inglewood, bringing CSJ values to the neighborhood and extraordinary service to the poor in the area. People on the streets knew that the doors of Daniel Freeman were never closed to the poor. But with the 1992 Los Angeles riots and the increasingly desperate condition of the poor in the area, together with the difficult health care situation, ministry at Daniel Freeman could no longer continue. In December 2001, the Daniel Freeman hospitals were sold to Tenet, a for-profit corporation, which in turn sold to Westridge Investment Corporation. Eventually in 2006, Memorial was closed, and the sisters moved out of the convent in November 2007. The spirit of the CSJ community at Daniel Freeman lives on, though, with a reunion of doctors, nurses, and all levels of employees twice a year.

When Sr. St. Claire Coyne ended her account of province history in 1966, the surge of new missions and increasing numbers of sisters was just at its peak. It was a time to look back and savor the growth and contribution of the sisters. "Today the Los Angeles province extends into five states, three archdioceses, nine dioceses; has 78 houses, staffs 70 elementary schools, with 479 sisters and 206 lay teachers; sixteen secondary schools with 146 Sisters of St. Joseph, 54 sisters of other communities, 43 priests, and 91 lay teachers; one college with a total faculty of 120 members—45 sisters and 75 lay instructors; five hospitals with 71 sisters on duty.

"It is well to remember that this inheritance was bequeathed to the present by Sisters of St. Joseph who braved remote, uncultured, Apache-infested territory in the latter part of the nineteenth century to found academies, hospitals, Indian schools, and an orphanage. They were the sole assistants of the few diocesan priests in the territory. It was the zealous, self-sacrificing devotion to duty on the part of the pioneer sisters together with their constant prayer and trust in God which enabled them to endure all the weariness, pain, fear, poverty, discouragement, and loneliness necessary to lay the foundations of the present flourishing province."[5]

CHAPTER 8

STIRRINGS OF CHANGE WITH VATICAN II

"But the parable that will be the most convincing is the one the sisters will write together, the parable of their lives."
                                        Design for Renewal

As large numbers of postulants continued to fill the novitiate, St. Mary's Academy was also stretching the limits of the campus, needing much more classroom and recreation space. In September 1953, the provincial wrote to the sisters, "With an increase of approximately one hundred students in the Academy we were forced to convert another dormitory into a classroom, thus eliminating more sleeping accommodations. Our chapel and refectory have long ago become inadequate so you see the House of Studies is an absolute necessity."

Dreams of moving the provincial headquarters and the novitiate began years earlier with, as always, special prayers to St. Joseph. Fundraising took on symbolic value at Christmas 1949 when a novice received a silver dollar as a Christmas gift. When Mother Rosemary, the provincial, was told of this silver dollar, she declared it to be the first dollar toward the new House of Studies. Sr. Mary Irene Flanagan, a first-year novice, created a little cotton pouch for the silver dollar, and hung it around the neck of the St. Joseph statue, where it stayed until the House of Studies opened in September 1955.[1]

Near to Mother Rosemary's heart was the dream of building St. Mary's House of Studies. As provincial, she oversaw the fund-raising, including appeals to families and benefactors. Sr. Helen Louise remembered, "Each house and individual sought different ways to contribute extra funds for the new buildings." Many learned how to make rosary beads to sell. "Someone in practically every convent/school taught piano before school, after school and at the noon hour, in order to bring in extra money." [2] When Mother Rosemary's term ended in 1953, she was appointed to oversee the planning and building of the House of Studies.

The site selected was on the lowest section of Mount St. Mary's College campus, overlooking the Los Angeles basin, the San Gabriel mountains, and miles of the Pacific Ocean. The architecture was modified Mediterranean with a Gothic arched cloister echoing the graceful design of the college buildings. The three-story, 75,000 square foot building seemed huge to those who had been living in the cramped quarters of St. Mary's Academy. Windows in the spacious parlors opened onto a beautiful garden, christened "the garth" by Sr. Francis Mary Rochefort, provincial treasurer. Refectory windows provided panoramic southern views of mountains and ocean. More important to the novices were the dormitories with individual sinks and closets for each person, and adjoining shower and tub rooms. Sr. Anne McMullen remembered, "Water was one of the greatest gifts of the new location, and we rejoiced in it." [3]

Grading the hill for the House of Studies

September 9, 1955, was moving day, and in the hurried activity, probably no one stopped to remember that this was the fifth move of the provincialate of the western province. The sisters had left the adobe house in Tucson in 1886 for the new St. Joseph's Academy on 15th Street. When the province was re-established in 1899, Mother Mary Elizabeth and Mother Julia decided on St. Mary's Academy on

21st and Grand in Los Angeles as province headquarters. Then in 1911, the fourth move was made to the new St. Mary's Academy on Slauson and Crenshaw.

In contrast to the earlier moves, the 1955 transfer to 11999 Chalon Road seemed to be of epic proportions. That summer had experienced an unbroken heat wave; it was 100 degrees on moving day. Sisters and novices, with the help of their fathers and brothers, packed and loaded furniture, beds, books, and equipment. Crews of

Moving day, September 9, 1955

novice-workers were bussed every day to the new building to clean, unpack, and arrange the rooms. A first-year novice remembered, "The day before moving day, beds and other pieces of furniture were hauled up to the new novitiate. The final night we slept on mattresses on the floor and felt like pioneers....We had lunch at noon on the green by the swimming pool and the professed sisters treated us to malts. After lunch we each got our suitcases and bedding and boarded the bus. It certainly was a strange sight to see more than ninety people moving out at once!" [4]

Accompanying the novices on September 9 were Mother

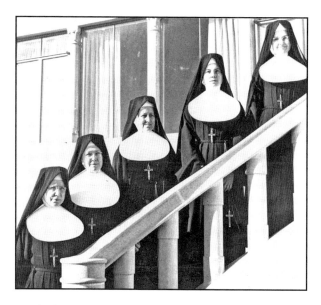

Leadership at new provincial center. From left Mother Rosaleen Lynch, Sisters Josephine Feeley, Roseanne Bromham, Rose Cecilia Harrington, Mary Joan Sexton

Roseanne Bromham, novice director, Sisters Rose Cecilia Harrington, postulant director, and Mary Joan Sexton, superior of the House of Studies community. A few days later on September 15, the doors of the House of Studies opened to welcome 61 young women to begin their postulancy. Finally, on September 29, the leadership group arrived—Mother Rosaleen Lynch, provincial superior, and Sisters Josephine Feeley, assistant provincial, Francis Mary Rochefort, provincial treasurer, and Mary Teresa Connelly, provincial secretary. Always present to make things happen was the tiny, dynamic Sr. Roberta Warren, assistant to the local superior. Adding to the local community of professed sisters were Sr. Monica Rose Wehner, in charge of the kitchen, and a small number of sisters doing graduate studies at nearby UCLA.

Marceline Mamake

"Marce and Edna"—two of our most faithful friends—came to us through one of our earliest ministries, our work with the Papago Indians at San Xavier del Bac Mission. Marceline Mamake was born in 1907 to parents living on a Papago reservation near San Xavier where our sisters had begun ministry three years after they arrived in Tucson.

When he was three years old, his mother died and his father brought him to San Xavier to be raised by the sisters. Marceline spent his early years at San Xavier, and then continued his education at St. Boniface School in Banning, California. When he graduated from high school, he could have chosen to return to the reservation where he would have become chief at his father's death. Instead, he stayed with the

(continued on next page)

sisters. It was to be a 73-year relationship with the Sisters of St. Joseph.

Marce's first job with the sisters was as driver and general handyman at St. Mary's Academy at Slauson and Crenshaw. A prominent role for Marce was to drive the blue St. Mary's bus which made many trips to the new site for Mount St. Mary's College in the Brentwood hills. But another destination was a life-changer for Marce. On Sunday mornings, he would drive a group of St. Mary's Academy girls to Blessed Sacrament Church where they sang the High Mass. Waiting by the bus for the girls to return, tall and handsome and shy, he attracted the attention of young Edna Calac, out walking her employers' dogs. They became friends, and three years later they were married, soon settling in a bungalow on the St. Mary's campus. Marce and Edna had one son, affectionately called "Little Chief", a treasured child who lived only six years.

During World War II, Marce served for two and a half years in the Air Force in India and China. He brought home a military commendation and medals as evidence of his part in the famous December 22-23, 1945 airlift of medical supplies "over the hump" between India and China.

The story of Marce and Edna was woven with the sisters' story over many years. When the novitiate and provincialate moved to the House of Studies in 1955, Marce and Edna were "missioned" there as well, moving into an apartment on the ground floor

Marce Mamake with his friend Sr. Roberta Warren

overlooking Santa Monica and the Pacific Ocean. As engineer and caretaker of the property, Marce kept everything working smoothly while he watched generations of sisters come and go. They remember his teasing smile and his quiet humor. He was sometimes encouraging, sometimes scolding, always gentle. Edna turned her energy to driving, claiming to having driven "millions of miles", including the day she took a group of CSJs to the port in San Pedro to leave for their first mission in Japan.

After Marce retired in 1972, they continued to live in their apartment at Carondelet Center, but spent time traveling and at their beloved ranch in Pauma Valley. In 1983, his health failing, Marce spent his last days receiving home care at Holy Family Community, attended by his loving Edna, the nurses, and his CSJ friends. Marce died on the morning of February 9, 1983, mourned by the many special ladies of his life. His funeral Mass in the big chapel at Carondelet Center was a celebration of resurrection hymns and tribal readings. The sisters knew they were saying goodbye to one of their most faithful friends, a part of their family.

They said goodbye to Edna soon after. She chose to live at their ranch in Pauma Valley, making rare visits to see the sisters. Edna Mamake died on March 20, 2001.

The move of the province center was complete, but one novice wrote, "moving to the House of Studies was like moving into a house with no furniture. I felt lonely. Each Saturday morning we would 'lie in wait' watching for the sisters who came by bus to the Mount for Saturday classes so we could wave to them." Another reminisced,

Study time for the novices. At center Sisters Marie Chapla and Merlynn Jane Martin

"It was strange to find ourselves without traditions, without history in this house. This was hard at first. We had joined the twentieth century—in the kitchen, laundry and dishroom. No more Elmer the potato peeler, potato cellar, antiquated laundry equipment, SMA plumbing! In place of the old wooden desks with lift-up lids (originally from the classrooms of SMA on Grand Avenue!), we had new metal desks!"[5]

The new House of Studies lacked only a chapel. Postulants, novices and professed sisters crowded for the first few years into a makeshift chapel set up in three adjoining classrooms. But building plans progressed rapidly, and the impressive structure began to take shape on the west side of the House of Studies, extending out over the access road to the college. The steady increase of numbers in the novitiate outpaced, however, the progress of the new chapel. With the large group of postulants in 1958, the classroom chapel became totally inadequate and services had to be moved into the unfinished chapel.

The dedication of St. Joseph's Chapel on March 30, 1959, was a solemn celebration with Cardinal James Francis McIntyre officiating and Auxiliary Bishop Timothy Manning delivering the sermon. Students of St. John's Seminary, directed by Fr. John Cremins, chanted the responses of the blessing, and the Mass was sung by the combined choir of postulants, novices, and junior professed sisters, directed by Sr. Miriam Joseph Larkin.

A great benefit of the novitiate move was its proximity to the college. With the novitiate just a short hike down the hill from the college, Mount faculty no longer had to travel to Slauson and Crenshaw to teach classes. On rare occasions, novices could produce their plays and entertainments in the Mount's Little Theater or on the stage of the Bowl. Novices from those first years have a treasured memory of one of the founders of the college, Sr. Dolorosa Mannix, old and frail, sitting in the novitiate to teach her class, constantly pushing her veil back from her face. (Legend had it that she never used the third veil pin, necessary to hold the folded-back veil in place.) She read to them very slowly, apologizing now and then for the slowness because she was translating from the Greek as she went. They remember this brilliant old nun, but not necessarily the class she was teaching.

Carondelet Center Chapel

Post-novitiate development of the sisters—spiritual, intellectual, and professional—was a high value with the Sisters of St. Joseph. As early as 1933, the first educational conference of the Sisters of St. Joseph of Carondelet was held in St. Paul, gathering sisters from all the provinces. The aim of the conference was to bring sisters of the congregation into closer relationships, correlate all phases of education work of the congregation, and encourage the development of sisters' literary talents. By the 1950s, sisters were being offered new opportunities for personal education and development. In 1954, Regina Mundi, an Institute of Sacred Studies for Religious Women, was established by the Sacred Congregation for Religious, offering a year of study in Rome. Sisters from all CSJ provinces were eligible to attend Regina Mundi, which was the only pontifical institute in Rome dedicated to providing theological formation for nuns and consecrated lay women. It served a good purpose in those years when women were not allowed into schools of theology in Rome. Later, when women began to be accepted worldwide in these fields of study, Regina Mundi closed, its usefulness ended.

Personal and spiritual renewal came closer home in 1957 when tertianship programs were begun in each province. Tertians—sisters professed from 15 to 20 years—spent six summer weeks withdrawn from their busy lives for spiritual renewal. In a spirit of quiet and recollection, the program included time for prayer and meditation, classes on theology, religious life and the vows, and discussion of issues important to these experienced sisters. A week of retreat completed the program. The Los Angeles tertianship, on the beautiful campus of the Academy of Our Lady of Peace in San Diego, began in 1957 with thirty-three sisters under the direction of Sr. Marie de Lourdes LeMay and Augustinian priest Fr. Charles J. Danaher, spiritual director. The program continued until 1969.

The juniorate, a two-year program of spiritual and professional formation following the novitiate, began in all the provinces in 1958, just a few years after the Sister Formation Program drew nationwide interest to the need for post-novitiate training in spiritual, intellectual, professional, and apostolic aspects of sisters' lives. The program was designed to include continuing education in theology and spirituality, professional and apostolic preparation, and a gradual transition into the professed life of the community. Many of the juniors chose their majors during this time and began work toward their degrees. In Los Angeles, establishing a juniorate meant creating space for newly professed sisters who would remain living at the House of Studies for an additional two years. With possible projections of sixty or more sisters, a new wing was needed. So the cycle began again—fundraising, architects, construction, resulting in the completion in 1959 of a four-story wing extending the House of Studies out to the south.

Space was not the only challenge when the juniorate began. In early summer of 1958, Mother Rosaleen had to inform pastors that she had fewer sisters to send out to teach. She wrote to a pastor in San Francisco, "Following the direction of Reverend Mother Eucharista, I have begun the juniorate for this province. This means that the sisters whom I would ordinarily be putting into the schools are not available to me this year….Though I am very sorry that it is necessary for me to do so, I am asking you, Father, to release one sister from [your] faculty. This will make a one-to-three ratio of lay teachers to sisters in your school."

Although the reality of having lay teachers in parish schools was becoming a little better understood, the financial impact on the school budget was a jolt to many pastors. At least one priest protested so vehemently that Reverend Mother Eucharista wrote attempting to explain. "It grieved me to know that you are unhappy about being requested to employ another lay teacher in your school….We know that some of our sisters now teaching are overworked because they are teaching without sufficient preparation and they are trying to get their credentials through attendance at Saturday classes and summer sessions….I fear this letter is no great solace to you, but I do believe that you will be happy to know that the girls from your school who made their vows last March will get this opportunity."

Those young sisters who made vows that March were pioneers. They had been the first group to enter at the hilltop House of Studies. Now, with construction going on all around them, thirty-four of them began the juniorate, tucked into every available space in the House of Studies. A trunkroom on the basement floor and a small sewing room became dormitories for some of the junior sisters—their belongings in their trunks placed next to their beds. Study space was scarce. Sisters remember studying in hallways, the laundry room, and practicing presentations in the tennis shoe room. Finally, by the fall of 1959, Sr. Sarah Marie Laubacher, the first juniorate superior, and the juniors were able to move into the new St. Joseph's Hall.

Over the years of the juniorate program, the horizons for preparation of the young sisters gradually broadened, along with the variety of ministries opening for religious. Choices of major fields increased, along with the use of other educational facililties, such as UCLA, USC, Daniel Freeman Hospital, and Los Angeles Trade Technical College. Juniors were attending lectures, concerts, and college activities, participating in college, parish, and archdiocesan committees, and becoming involved in volunteer work. With these increasing options for post-novitiate development, the decrease in vocations during the 1960s, and the fact that young women were now required to have several years of education or work experience before entering the community, the decision was made in 1970 to close the Los Angeles juniorate program.

The 1950s had been a decade filled with stirrings of change and renewal. During Mother Eucharista Galvin's two terms as superior general from 1954-1966, the congregation looked at the spiritual and professional needs of the sisters, resulting in programs like tertianship, the juniorate, and congregational exchanges among colleges and hospitals. With her broad vision of the needs of the church, she was a leader in laying the groundwork for the American Federation of the Sisters of St. Joseph and in establishing the Conference of Major Superiors of Women which became, in 1971, the Leadership Conference of Women Religious.

Responding to Pope Pius XII's appeal to large communities to send members to the foreign missions, Mother Eucharista traveled to Japan to identify possible ministry sites. The result was the arrival on August 14, 1956 of four sisters of St. Joseph in Yokohama Harbor. The first Los Angeles sisters to serve in the Japan missions were Sisters Eva Francis Cereghino and Barbara Mary Sanborn. Six years later in 1962, at the call of Pope John XXIII for religious communities to send ten per cent of their members as missionaries to Latin America, another group of sisters, including Sisters Mary Arthur Meyer, Therese Donahue, and Teresa Avalos from the Los Angeles Province, arrived in Peru.

More change came with the 15th General Chapter of 1960 which was preceded for the first time by chapters in each province. Community prayers were to be revised and said in English, rather than the traditional Latin. Provision was made for annual vacations, and rules of silence were relaxed for some occasions. Minor modifications in the habit included replacing shawls with heavy coats for sisters living in cold climates. A groundbreaking permission for selected sisters to drive automobiles may have drawn more excited attention than the formal approvals of the juniorate, tertianship, and preparation for missions in South America.

In the midst of these changing times, Pope John XXIII was elected as successor to Pius XII on October 28, 1958. Elderly, genial, and undoubtedly considered an interim pope, John XXIII soon stunned the church by announcing the second Vatican Council with the memorable words that it was time to open the windows to let in some fresh air. Vatican II began officially on October 11, 1962, addressing issues deeply affecting the church and the world, and opening four years of intense interest and dialogue. Over these years, the faithful pondered pronouncements issuing from some of the goals of the Council—defining the nature of the church in the modern world, renewing the church, and developing a dialogue with the contemporary world.

Providing context to the Council's pronouncements, Pope John issued two powerful encyclicals during his short years as head of the Church. *Mater et Magistra* (1961) commemorated the 70th anniversary of Pope Leo XIII's *Rerum Novarum* and other papal writings on social teaching. *Pacem in Terris*, signed by John a few months before he died in 1963, dealt with world peace, human rights, and resolving conflicts with negotiation rather than arms. The teaching of these encyclicals on working toward authentic community, promoting human dignity, and becoming involved in social justice issues had a particularly profound impact on women and men religious.

On October 28, 1965, in its last year, the Council published the *Decree on the Renewal of Religious Life*, known by the first two words of the decree *Perfectae Caritatis* (in perfect charity). The opening paragraph of the decree states its purpose: "to deal with the life and discipline of those institutes whose members make profession of chastity, poverty and obedience, and to make provision for their needs, as our times recommend." Because of the wide diversity of institutions, the council gave authority to each group to make concrete decisions on renewal, but specified that renewal should follow the double movement necessary for renewal of the Church—fidelity to God's revealed Word and greater adaptation to the needs of the present. For religious communities, God's revealed Word was to be found not only in the Gospel, but also in the inspiration of the founder in the primitive documents. Communities were to adapt to the needs of modern life and to the situations where the sisters lived and worked.

The Vatican Council's call for renewal resonated in the congregation. Sisters were reading and discussing the decrees and directives from Rome, and anticipating congregational directives to come. In just six months, the 16th General Chapter convened in St. Louis on April 28, 1966, with the aim of revitalizing every phase of life in the congregation, eliminating obsolete customs, revising the Constitution, and providing more flexible structures of community life with a deep concern for the personal, social, communal, and apostolic life of the sisters. Chapter recessed on May 3, and reconvened a year and a half later from November 18-December 1, 1967. By the end of this second session, the general chapter, the highest authority in the congregation, had published *Design for Renewal of the Sisters of St. Joseph*, stating that the "decrees as contained…constitute the norms by which the Sisters of St. Joseph of Carondelet will live until these norms are altered by a later chapter. These decrees have the same binding force that the approved Constitutions held."[6]

Asserting the relevance of religious life to today's world, *Design for Renewal* laid out in contemporary language the principles of religious life, beginning with the purpose and the end of the Congregation and the public profession of the vows of poverty, chastity, and obedience. In the first pages, the *Design* broadened the vision of the ministry of the congregation. "It is the special task of the Sisters of St. Joseph to share Christ's mission through serving His Church: to teach, to help the sick and needy, to be a sacrament of His mercy in the world. It is their challenge to discover, through listening to the Word and also to the world, new parables: new ways of announcing the Good News of Christ so that the [people] of this day will listen and understand."[7]

In the next twenty-eight pages of this groundbreaking little volume, changes and modifications to the traditional lives of the sisters were laid out. Sisters were reminded of their important role in the quality of local community, in their practice of a more contemporary understanding of obedience, and in governance of the province. Experimentation was encouraged in electing local superiors, small group living, group government, and budgeting, A representative assembly with elected delegates was to be set up in every province.

Design for Renewal affirmed the importance of communal prayer, while allowing the individual sisters ample time for personal prayer and longer periods of spiritual renewal. A house of prayer was to be established in the congregation. The section on formation included the importance of fostering good personal relationships, studying the social encyclicals, and combining orientation to community living with apostolic experience and education.

A recurring theme in the *Design* was that of leaving many choices to the individual. Sisters had the option of returning to their baptismal names if they wished, and many did. In the case of religious dress, the General Chapter left to the individual sister the choice of retaining the traditional habit or changing to contemporary religious dress. "…Both the traditional habit and modern forms of religious dress seem to have a message for contemporary Americans. It is for this reason that the Congregation, through the General Chapter, is providing a choice of dress for its members. Those who choose to wear the familiar habit of a Sister of St. Joseph do so as an affirmation of their belief in its positive values and as a tribute to the many sisters who have worn it with dignity….The sisters who elect contemporary religious dress wear it as a sign that religious life is relevant to today's men and women and that Sisters of St. Joseph have a positive role to play in the shaping of a better world." [8]

Of all the anticipated outcomes of the chapter's actions, religious dress had probably been the most volatile topic. Then came the stunning decision of giving each person the choice of her religious dress. This seemed a symbolic gesture, placing the individual sister on a whole different plane. Now she was to take responsibility not only for dress, but also for her social behavior, prayer, ministry, even the choice of changing her name. A Sister of St. Joseph reminisced recently about the experience, first describing an earlier directive that came down from the Generalate that the long rosary would no longer be worn with the habit. Sisters were to remove the rosary immediately upon reading the letter. Compare, then, her experience of reading in *Designs for Renewal* that she was free to choose how she would dress in the future! She was being invited now to a future of decision-making and participation in a profoundly changed community of the Sisters of St. Joseph, one still securely rooted in the original charism of the founders, but adapted now to the needs of the times and to the situations where the sisters lived and worked.

CHAPTER 9

SERVING A CHANGING CULTURE

"It worried me, but I realized that if we were going to serve a changing culture, we'd have to be a part of it."

Reverend Mother Eucharista

The congregation had given a clear message about change in *Design for Renewal*, but the bigger tasks remained—communication, education, and implementation. As the process of renewal began in early 1968, the Los Angeles Province numbered 894 sisters—strong individuals, educated, thoughtful, and diverse, scattered widely across the western United States. Big plans were needed. Under the leadership of Sr. Mary Brigid Fitzpatrick, provincial superior from 1968 to 1974, renewal got underway.

A first step toward renewal was the formation in 1968 of an elected government group—the Sisters Representative Assembly (SRA)—with the purpose of giving the sisters a direct share in the government of the province. As an advisory group to the Provincial Council, the SRA developed a government plan, set up working committees, and encouraged the sisters to share their concerns and proposals. Minutes of an early SRA meeting defined one aspect of the sisters' direct share as encouraging "creative thinking in developing forward-looking proposals and projects regarding the future of religious life in the Congregation in its service to the Church."

Structures began to emerge. A committee was already functioning in the province to study the needs of sisters in pre-retirement and retirement years. A Local Community Living Study was initiated in the province by 1968, an Apostolic Board was established the next year to give direction to ministry in the province, and a Judicial Council was set up in 1970 to mediate sisters' concerns. By January 1970, CSJs were being invited by the SRA to volunteer for membership in three secretariats—Government, Social Action, and Spiritual Renewal. A fourth secretariat on the Future was established a few years later.

Retreats were an early interest of spiritual renewal. Weekend retreats at the House of Studies were among the first options offered. As early as 1968, a selection of small retreats on a variety of themes began to replace the traditional large annual retreats at the college and other province institutions. In August of 1971, a two-week renewal program was planned in response to "an overwhelming number of requests from the sisters for a shared spiritual experience open to all."[1] A total of 650 sisters gathered at six locations from Our Lady of Peace in San Diego to Dominican College in San Rafael; presenters traveled in teams of two to the various sites.

Planners reached for outstanding leaders in post-conciliar thought, including Jesuit priests James Gill of Harvard, James McPolin of the Biblical Institute of Rome, and Robert McNally of Fordham. Other presenters were Father Thomas More Newbold of the Catholic Theological Union in Chicago, Fr. William McNamara of Sedona Renewal and Ecumenical Center, and Dr. Ruth Hoffman, professor of sociology at Mount St. Mary's College.

The letter inviting the sisters shows how the spirit of renewal shaped the workshop. "In post-conciliar times examination and evaluation have called for appraisal of weaknesses and needs. This activity could breed discouragement. We are fortunate in having a program planned in a spirit of hope. It can deepen our prayers, help us to value anew our commitment to God and lead us to move with wisdom and courage into our varied works for others. Let us all keep these coming days of grace in our prayers, asking that the Holy Spirit may come upon the speakers, and upon us all."

By May 1974, a province renewal team had been established to work with individuals and local communities to "better their communication with each other, to help them in community and shared prayer and in the expression of the common goals of religious life."[2] Sisters Rita Angerman and Carmen de la Vega were appointed full-time team coordinators. Part-time members were Sisters Rose Cecilia Harrington, Joan Henehan, Anne McMullen, and Barbara Sullivan.

The Secretariat and the renewal team, enthusiastically supported in the province, produced an impressive list of activities. Three weeks of theological education and reflection were offered with an Institute of Spirituality in summer 1974 with Father John Lozano CMF, the St. Louis Province renewal team, and Los Angeles sister presenters. Topics ranged from theology of community to history of apostolic life, spirit of the founder, spiritual reading, and prayer. In 1975, Father John Conway, CM, spent the entire year traveling throughout the province giving renewal days and weekends to provide common experience in religious consecration and spirituality.

By the mid-1970s, sisters could choose from a wide selection of retreats—directed, preached, and private. Thirty-day retreats were available for those who wished. Workshops were offered in topics like discernment, biblical spirituality, contemporary theology of the vows, Myers-Briggs, and spiritual direction. In 1978, Villa Maria House of Prayer opened in La Habra, California, and the Mount St. Mary's College Spirituality Center opened on the Doheny Campus.

Early staff of Villa Maria House of Prayer. From left Marcia Obloy, Sisters Thomas Bernard MacConnell, Eleanor Wagner, Veronica Maloney, Leone LaPorte

This program was followed by the Archdiocesan Spirituality Center in 1983 offering direction and support for those desiring to grow in spirituality and to receive training for ministry in spiritual direction.

During these years of education and conversation about consecrated life, members acknowledged that issues in the life of the province needed to be named and dealt with. Sr. Mary Seraphine, superior general, had written to the congregation on January 15, 1968: "Community living cannot continue unless the peace of God is present. Pope John XXIII opened a door but each of us must open another before the spirit of the Chapter and the Vatican Council can permeate and fill each house. That opening may require the demolition of walls of prejudice, pride, self-satisfaction, self-will, everything that prevents each sister from being accepted as she is. This may well be a call to battle with oneself to bring to light a depth of understanding, a warmth of compassion, and a capacity for love for the other members of the community."

Design for Renewal had set forth values necessary for renewal in community living—quality of local community, contemporary understanding of obedience and governance, importance of personal and communal prayer, improved communication, good personal relationships—and had invited experimentation in small group living. By 1969, proposals were being submitted through the SRA to the Provincial Council for experimental group living. Carondelet High School and convent

Cardinal James Francis McIntyre, Sr. Mary Brigid Fitzpatrick, provincial, with Mother Mary Seraphine, superior general

began a unique experiment that year allowing the school principal, in consultation with the regional superior, to select her new faculty from CSJ volunteers. The group began the year with a weekend together, praying, discussing their goals and expectations for community, and choosing authority centered in the group as their form of government. In a report at the end of the first year, the group emphasized the importance of communication. "Since we realized the need for group discussion on a regular basis, we set aside every Monday evening for a community meeting. These discussions have made us more aware of the meaning and necessity of authority, leadership, accountability and shared decision-making."

The Carondelet High School group, innovative as it was, had followed the traditional type of community living with all members assigned to a common ministry. Other early experimental groups drew sisters from a variety of ministries. Holy Spirit community, living in a rented house on Alvarado Terrace in Los Angeles, was composed of four sisters from the college, one from St. Mary's Academy, one from St. Jerome's School, and two sisters in graduate study. This community later relocated to St. Clement's convent in Venice, beginning a long CSJ presence in that parish. Villa Carondelet in Tucson had an even more diverse mix of ministries, including a retired sister.

The Nativity Parish community in Torrance was another early experimental group, bringing together nine sisters who had been assigned to large institutional communities. As they developed their goals for community living, these sisters also committed themselves to volunteer service of the parish contributing scripture study, liturgy planning, and health-related and clerical assistance. Parishioners deeply appreciated the presence of the sisters and the knowledge and experience they shared.

A few years after Nativity community began, four of their members, embracing the same goals but with emphasis on simplicity of life, became the core group of Casa Esperanza community established in south central Los Angeles. This community developed a statement of goals which has been maintained through the years of its existence.

We, as a Community of Hope, strive to:
celebrate life and the unexpected
deepen our experience of God
share the life we have
seek after justice
live in visible simplicity
share what we are and what we have
reach out to those in need
reverence, support and encourage one another.

Casa Esperanza community 1974. Front row from left Sisters Jeannette Van Vleck, Louise Bernstein, Rose Cecilia Harrington. Second row from left Sisters Callista Roy, Consuelo Aguilar, Marilyn Schafer, Annette Debs, Rosaleen Russell. Standing Sr. Julie Marciacq

These were not small changes. The departure of some of the sisters from traditional convent living had to be painful and hard for many to understand. There were strong feelings of rejection and diminishment. Communication about commonly held values was extraordinarily difficult. It was hard to trust. One of the groups in the 1971 renewal program had written to the Provincial Council of their increasing awareness of grave problems stemming from inadequate communication. "Our speakers not only identified but confirmed this condition as serious throughout the province....This faulty communication is moving us toward greater polarity, possibly leading to division in the community we love." Improvement of communication on the common goals of religious life had become a major component of the province renewal program, but there was a long way to go.

A New and Welcoming Community

On October 15, 1985, the anniversary of the founding of the Sisters of St. Joseph, the province welcomed the gift of four sisters transfering from the Vietnamese congregation of the Daughters of Mary Immaculate. After a long perilous journey to an unknown future, Sisters Simon Hoang, Flavie Nguyen, Marie Juliette Nguyen, and Eugenia Phan, along with Sr. Eugenia's elderly parents, had found their home with the Sisters of St. Joseph. Sr. Eugenia told the story of this journey of faith.[3]

The Vietnamese Sisters of Mary Immaculate at their transfer to the Sisters of St. Joseph of Carondelet, 1986. From left Sisters Flavie Nguyen, Eugenia Phan, Marie Juliette Nguyen, Simon Hoang

"At the beginning of 1975, the American bases in Vietnam closed, one after another. The rockets fired by the Communists into the cities came more and more often. We knew that the end was coming and all the people were in a panic. In March 1975, our community moved along with the people into the South. In April, we had a meeting to consider our future and how to face this event." Believing the Communists would not let them live in community, they decided to separate and live in small groups. Whoever had families could go to live with them. If the parents had a way to leave the country, the sister could go with them.

"After this decision, we said goodbye to each other with tears in our eyes, and we left to find some place to live. We had a little money which the community gave to us. By the end of April, there was no communication between cities. We knew the end had come."

(continued on next page)

On the morning of April 19, friends came to tell them they had a way to get out. "Our problem was how to get to the boat which would conduct us to the ship. Between our location and the water there was a high, steep cliff. The descent to the boat was hazardous and we knew that at any moment enemy rockets would be coming our way. Holding our breath and concentrating, we slowly climbed down the cliff." Finally they reached the small boat that would take them out to the Navy ship waiting offshore. It took three hours in rough seas to reach the ship.

"From our small boat roughly tossed by the waves, we had to climb up into the ship by means of a rope ladder stretching down two stories to our boat. Finally, with God's help, and a fearful struggle, we were on board." Many of their belongings they had tried to bring with them didn't make it up that long rope ladder. Sr. Eugenia remembered losing hold of the little book of the Constitutions of her religious community and watching it fall back into the water.

Their journey brought them first to Guam and finally to California, where 17,000 Vietnamese refugees were in temporary shelter at Camp Pendleton. That was where they met Sr. Evelyn Joseph Flynn, currently ministering in the diocesan mission office, who was searching out priests and sisters among the refugees. She described the scene in a letter. "It took many trips to Camp Pendleton to unearth all of the religious. One has to remember the confusion of those days—new refugees coming in every day—loud speakers calling out day and night in Vietnamese while relative tried to find relative, and friend find friend."

Sr. Eugenia continued the story. "One day, Sr. Evelyn Joseph, CSJ, came and had a meeting with all the nuns. After the meeting, we asked her to sponsor our group." Soon the Los Angeles Province took the little group to their heart, offering sponsorship for the sisters and for Sr. Eugenia's aged parents—providing them with a living situation in community, financial support and education, and always respecting their identity as a Vietnamese religious community.

Sr. Eugenia's parents lived at Carondelet Center until their deaths. A few of the sisters left for Connecticut to be with parents. The remaining four found ministry and homes in the province, becoming Sisters of St. Joseph in 1985. Many were reminded how history repeats itself. Sisters of St. Joseph escaped the terrors of the French Revolution sheltered by generous friends and family, and our Vietnamese sisters fled the chaos of the final days of the Vietnam war, and found a home with a new and welcoming community.

The years from the beginning of renewal through the 1970s saw division and tension in the community. "Anything that caused division, anything that created a we/they situation was divisive and very difficult—change of habit, prayer styles, ministry, life style, social justice issues. We did not know how to really talk with each other—really communicate—and it was difficult to begin."[4] Despite efforts to improve communication, many sisters tended to feel judged, isolated, excluded.

Large numbers left the community during these years. There were many reasons for these departures as Sr. Sandra Schneiders pointed out in her Women and Spirit Lecture in September, 2011. The second Vatican Council had clarified the universal call to holiness and ministry, which was no longer assumed to be the exclusive role of religious. Some realized at this midpoint of their lives that their real motives for becoming a religious had been the desire for deeper spirituality and the ability to minister in the Church. It was possible and acceptable now to serve the Church and the world outside religious life.

Other reasons for leaving the community were more personal. For some, the changes in the congregation were not welcome; for some they were too slow, or too fast. Sometimes it was old angers or disappointments that surfaced and became causes for action. For each sister, the decision to leave was deeply personal. Sr. Mary Brigid, provincial superior during the 1970s, pointed out that "each sister had to reconsider her vocation, her bond with community and membership, to grow in greater clarity about who she was, why she was here, what God was asking of her." Sister Mary Brigid saw it as God calling these sisters to leave.[5] "Inner structures began to oppose outer structures," said another former provincial superior. "Those who stayed became stronger."[6]

Sisters Rosanne Bromham and Mary Anne Bahner ring the bell at St. Mary's Academy.

Studies in the changing habit: faculty and sisters in residence at the new St. Mary's Academy, Inglewood, 1968-69

Probably the most distracting and painful issue during this time was the change of religious dress. But as the sisters began to change their appearance, and sober-toned suits and dresses evolved into more contemporary styles and colors, the novelty faded and attention turned to a more compelling topic. From the late 1960s, the total numbers of sisters in the Los Angeles Province had begun to decline. Numbers of young women entering the novitiate had decreased sharply during the 1960s. Now at the end of the decade, with deaths of elderly sisters and with departures of members in both temporary and permanent vows, community numbers were steadily decreasing.[7] With fewer sisters available for the traditional works of the community, the province soon faced critical decisions about ministry.

The minutes of a joint meeting of the Provincial Council and the Apostolic Board in December 1970 describe "a crisis situation—a major personnel shortage." Although the congregation's commitment to give effective service to the Church was unchanged, the province's call to respond to the personnel crisis required immediate action. The focus needed to be on the total needs of the province, building vitality into more concentrated service. This meant reducing numbers of sisters in some CSJ-staffed schools, and total withdrawal from others. CSJ principals drew up criteria for possible withdrawal from schools. Regional superiors now had the responsibility of meeting with pastors and parents, bishops and school supervisors, to assess the school's situation: which school could continue without the sisters, which had a promising educational future, which might bear a particular witness to school integration. Wrenching decisions had to be made and carried out.

There had been a few school closures in the late 1960s, three in 1969 including Holy Cross and St. Patrick's in Los Angeles, and Villa Carondelet High School in Tucson, formerly St. Joseph's Academy founded in 1870. All three were cherished schools tied to the early history of the province, and losing them was painful. But beginning in 1971, the province experienced years of heartbreaking withdrawals and school closures, averaging from two to six each year. From 1971 to 2000, the community withdrew from a total of 58 schools all along the west coast. Sister teachers were saying goodbye to networks of old friends and former students in these parishes, and wondering about the future of what had been the primary ministry of the western province up to this time.

New creative ministries, meanwhile, were emerging as beacons of hope even in the landscape of school withdrawals. Holy Cross Middle School, for instance, initiated an inter-parochial education plan in the Los Angeles Archdiocese. A team of eight CSJs led by their first principal, Sr. Patricia Zins, consolidated grades seven and eight of six neighboring parish schools in 1969. Occupying the buildings of the former Holy Cross elementary school in the heart of south-central Los Angeles, the middle school flourished for thirty years until, because of decreasing enrollment, it had to close in 1999.

In 1973, a young sister in Tucson saw a need that she could not turn away from, and began a groundbreaking ministry to abused children. Sr. Kathleen Clark told the story herself. "It all started with my first impression of child abuse in the worst form. One evening in 1958, while I was working at St. Mary's Hospital as night supervisor, a three-year-old girl was brought in who was the most severely injured victim of abuse I had ever seen. The child had been sadistically tortured since birth….She was starving….This was my first experience with the horrible plight of children who are utterly helpless at the hands of their own parents." [8]

This experience led Sr. Kathleen to establish La Casa de los Niños

Crisis Center in a house on a busy boulevard in Tucson. For her, it was a lifelong mission. As Sr. Kathleen's ideas developed, she saw beyond the need to care for these abused children. A welcoming home was needed where parents in crisis and at risk could bring their children to keep them safe from abuse. This would be a voluntary program of prevention. She explained, "The Casa was created to provide a temporary home with loving care for infants of parents who are momentarily unable to cope with their responsibilities and who need relief while they resolve personal problems."[9] Services were to be free with no questions asked. "All they have to do is come to my front door."

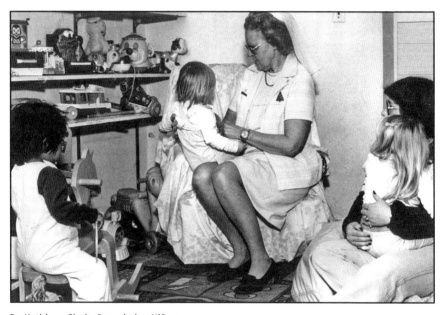

Sr. Kathleen Clark, Casa de los Niños

Sr. Kathleen's initial idea was to develop crisis nurseries in several parts of the city near hospitals and service agencies. "But the hippies and motorcycle gangs who were leading her to many of the abused babies convinced her to change her plan. 'They said that none of the people they knew would trust us if we were next to places like that. They led me into big drainage pipes where families were living. People began bringing children to us that they couldn't care for on their own. They trusted us to take care of them until things improved.'" [10]

One of the first crisis prevention nurseries in the nation, the Casa hit a nerve with Tucson. When Sr. Kathleen opened the doors with $17 in her pocket in 1973, she was prepared for eighteen children. "By the end of the first week, we had 26," she said. "I was frantic for help, so I called some of the fraternities at the university. Well, 12 to 18 big guys came over and they were sitting all over the floor, feeding babies." [11] Three years later, the Casa had cared for over 1700 children. In the years to come, as its services expanded, thousands of children were sheltered, parent education programs established, and families reunited. [12]

From its beginning, independent of federal or state funding, the Casa operated with a core staff paid through contributions, and with the help of hundreds of volunteers. Sr. Kathleen welcomed the help of all without distinction—friends and neighbors, churches of all faiths, service clubs, and interested people, including her CB Radio Operators club who named her "Kid Sister" and the local Hell's Angels in town ("angels are angels") who helped with donations and fund-raisers.

Sr. Kathleen's model of preventing child abuse was widely duplicated nation-wide. Sr. Ann Weltz, her co-worker at the Casa, brought the concept to California establishing the Bay Area Crisis Nursery in 1981 in the city of Concord. Like the Casa, this crisis nursery offers free, voluntary, and confidential services, and is funded by private donations. Additional services include a second shelter for older children, ages six through eleven, and a Respite Care program allowing monthly respite care of children whose parents need time to reach out for additional services for stress reduction. This program, the only one of its kind in the San Francisco Bay area, has logged well over 20,000 admissions.

The Bay Area Crisis Nursery's slogan—"a little heart, a little help, a lot of hope"—can speak for many ministries of the Sisters of St. Joseph over the years, beginning with the Indian missions, orphan homes, work with the deaf, schools and hospitals. The slogan still speaks of CSJ mission for the new ministries taking shape in the years following the call of *Design for Renewal*.

Chapter 10

New ways of announcing the Good News

"It is their challenge to discover, through listening to the Word and also to the world, new parables: new ways of announcing the Good News of Christ."

Design for Renewal

Listening to the signs of the times in the 1960s and 1970s brought clear messages. Freedom rides and marches for civil rights, riots burning the cities, heartbreaking assassinations, an endless war in Vietnam draining the nation of hope, a disgraced Presidency—it was clear the world was ready to hear good news.

The clear success of one woman's crusade with Casa de los Niños helped pave the way for other CSJ efforts to respond to the needs of the world with the Good News. Three new ministries in the early 1970s caught the imagination of the community and proved to be prophetic of the future. In 1973, sisters joined César Chávez in Delano, California, to live and work directly with the farmworkers. A year later, Sisters Clare Dunn and Judith Lovchik began a political ministry in Arizona. And in 1976, St. Joseph's Center started a long history of direct service to the poor in Venice, California. Many of the CSJ works founded in later years took heart and shape from these groundbreaking innovations.

In the summer of 1973, six CSJs from Los Angeles came to the heart of California's San Joaquin valley to help out where they could in the grapeworkers' struggle for human rights. Working directly with César Chávez, founder of the United Farm Workers, they brought what they had—their gifts, professional training, and, most important, their presence as women religious. Sisters Mary Ann Sandoval, Loretta Marie Hibbard, and Judy Lovchik worked in the Coachella offices of the Salad Bowl strike which eventually won higher wages for workers in the grape and lettuce fields. Sr. Linda Snow was a laboratory technician in the Delano clinic. Sr. Louise Bernstein, who was bilingual, was a receptionist in a Salinas clinic and did home visiting and translating, and Sr. Anne Gertrude Fitzgerald worked in the business office of UFW headquarters in Keene.

CSJ volunteers in the central valley. First row from left Sisters Aileen Francis Pidge, Clare Dunn, Louise Bernstein, Judith Lovchik, Marilyn Schafer. Standing from left Sisters Julie Marciacq, Jeanette Van Vleck, Mary Ann Sandoval, Patricia Sears, Joan Viery, Toni Nash.

The presence of the sisters became even more significant that summer when over 300 persons were arrested in Fresno for protesting in the interests of the farmworkers. On July 31 at 11:50 a.m., a message came into the office of the provincial superior, Sr. Mary Brigid: Phone message from Sr. Joan of United Farm Workers. Urgent—will call back at 2 or 2:30 p.m. At 2:30, Sr. Mary Brigid wrote down this second message. "Phone call from Sr. Joan. Sr. Rose

Cecilia asked her to contact me to say that she was among the group of sisters and priests arrested at 9 a.m. today. They chose to act in opposition to ordinance that pickets stand 100' apart and bullhorns not be used. They stood in groups and used bullhorns. They wish to remain in jail until everyone is released on own recognizance."

Sisters Rose Cecilia Harrington, Joan Viery, and Rachel Fitzgerald of the Los Angeles Province, and Annabelle Raiche, a CSJ general councilor from St. Paul, were among the 14 women religious, 16 priests, and a Methodist minister jailed for two weeks. These sisters were not the first CSJs to be imprisoned for their beliefs—Mother St. John Fontbonne, second founder of the congregation, was imprisoned and narrowly escaped the guillotine during the French Revolution—and were not the last. But this act of defiance of injustice marked a symbolic moment in the journey of the Sisters of

---

Reflections on a summer experience, August 1973

"Lord, it is good for us to be here." This is the thought more than any other which I constantly returned to during the time I spent in a Fresno prison because of my support of the United Farmworkers' cause. With this thought came the awesome realization that it was part of the Lord's plan for me to sharpen, intensify and compress into a two-week period experiences basic to my life as a Sister of St. Joseph—

–to be physically limited, confined and monitered and yet to know great freedom of spirit

– to be utterly deprived and yet to experience deliverance from need

– to discover that because everyone was forced to seek solitude in the same place it could be found in the midst of community

– and in fact to recognize the solidarity of that community as stemming from a common cause and goal, not from common background or work

– to experience the powerful sustenance that is prayer, whether the Word is read first in Spanish, then in English, or the evening rosary, or the simple awareness of a reconciling presence of the celebration of the Eucharist at the end of each day

– to sense the support of the many who responded in person or in spirit to "I was in prison and you visited me" and to know that though I was only one, those who cared were many.

Complete identification with the poor is an impossibility as long as it is a matter of choice. But it is possible to make a decision which implies a sharing with the "least of the brethren" to the extent that God determines. I thought that I was making that decision early one morning in the park at Parlier. I came to realize during the days that followed that the decision was a gift and I was the receiver. I am grateful.

Sr. Rose Cecilia Harrington

St. Joseph of Carondelet after the second Vatican Council.

The protesters were released in August when their cases were dismissed. Some of the summer workers went home to their regular ministries, but others stayed to work, primarily in the clinics. Sisters Theresa Kvale began service as a nurse in Delano and Keene, and Aileen Francis Pidge worked in a Delano pharmacy. Sisters Mary Conroy was a lab technician in Salinas clinic, and Joan Viery worked in a hiring hall.

Casa de Amigos community, Delano, 1973. From left Sisters Theresa Kvale, Joan Viery, Aileen Francis Pidge, Linda Snow

Later, the sisters reflected, "I felt it was time to narrow the gap between theory and practice, time to 'get our hands dirty.'" Actively involved with the grapeworkers in their lives, including the picketing of the fields and living on the same $15 a week, "it was good to simply be with the farmworkers. The presence of religious means a great deal to them. It is important for all the world to see the Church visibly assisting the oppressed and identifying with them in their struggle for justice, for basic human rights....I gave of myself to the people and in return they taught me a lot about what it really means to be poor." [1]

In the 1980s, Sr. Maria Angela Mesa developed the Hispanic Apostolate Office in the Fresno diocese, and planned ways to serve the workers. Forty parish evangelization teams regularly visited up to eighty camps where young workers sat on the grass or leaned against walls after a long day in the fields to share faith and the sacraments, worker to worker. Emphasis was on the dignity of the person, preparation of leaders in the little towns, and growth in

Sr. Maria Angela Mesa

understanding of the Church. The evangelization teams visited the camps sharing information, faith, word and sacrament. They walked a thin line. In Maria Angela's words, "They did not only 'churchy' things with them but also helped restore their sense of worth and dignity as human persons through social and political information."

Acutely conscious of the farmworkers' need to learn English, Sr. Maria Angela recruited Sr. Constance Fitzgerald to teach them. Sr. Constance created English as a second language materials for the group of workers at Blackwell Corner, a permanent labor camp 100 miles southwest of Fresno. "Each week I spent two days at the camp, taught women at home during the day and had two classes in the evening for the field workers. Because of their sensitivity and loving concern, the farmworkers suggested that the first evening class be held as soon as the men and women came from work, with delayed supper, so that I would not be too late driving alone back to Fresno."[2]

César Chávez always appreciated the Sisters of St. Joseph, early supporters of his cause. In 1975, he wrote to Sr. Mary Kevin Ford, general superior: "On this, the second anniversary of the beginning of the Coachella grape strike, I would like to express to you the farmworkers' appreciation for all that the Sisters of your Community are doing with us....These sisters have given tirelessly of themselves – not only of their boundless physical energy, but most importantly to us, of their spirits and their prayer and the example of their lives. They came to us during difficult times and they have stayed with us – sacrificing as we do, struggling with us to achieve justice and respect for our own human dignity. Because they are here, we know the strength of the support of your entire Community's prayer." [3]

Six sisters of St. Joseph were among the thousands in the three-hour, six-mile march to César Chávez's funeral liturgy in Delano in May 1993. Two served as Eucharistic ministers, representing the 20-year history of the Sisters of St. Joseph with César and the farmworkers, a beacon for many in the province pointing out the acute needs of the poor.

The year after the sisters joined César Chávez in San Joaquin Valley, a new CSJ ministry was initiated—working and educating for social justice through legislative action. Sisters Clare Dunn and Judith Lovchik were responding to the 1971 Synod of Bishops statement: "Action on behalf of justice and participation in the transformation of the world fully appear to us as a constitutive dimension of preaching the Gospel." The call had come as well from the congregation. The General Chapter of 1972 had recommended:

Protest march, 1970s

"That each sister be encouraged to engage actively—according to her particular interests, knowledge, and abilities—in those areas of political life which are instrumental in promoting Gospel-oriented social changes."

In January 1974, Sr. Clare asked permission from the community to run for political office in Arizona's House of Representatives. Although the community was faithfully following the way of Vatican II, giving concrete form to the ideals proved to be complex and painful. Because of the uniqueness of the request, and because it involved the compatibility of religious life with electoral office and service of the religious in the Church, both the provincial and the general councils discussed the request. The bishops of Tucson and Phoenix were consulted, Tucson's Bishop Green stating that he would not endorse her, but had no objections. Bishop McCarthy of Phoenix had a stronger objection, saying that although he could not forbid her to pursue electoral office, he had serious reservations regarding the role of a religious in partisan politics. After several months of study, prayer, and consultation, the Provincial Council decided in March that they could not approve Sr. Clare's request.

Letters began to come in from CSJs and from representatives of national organizations of priests and religious expressing objections to the Council's decision. In late April, Clare wrote an open letter to the Council asking to meet with them. "The Council members met with Sr. Clare and thirteen sisters on the morning of May 20th. It was a painful meeting, but many issues surfaced which we must honestly face as a province in the months and years ahead. Some of these are: authority, ministry, Church, plurality and diversity, and the decision-making process. It was at this same meeting that Sr. Clare made known her great difficulty in accommodating her conscience to the Council decision in her regard." In the end, Sr. Mary Brigid took the only option she felt she could offer Sr. Clare. "I have taken the position that I neither endorse nor support her filing for candidacy for a seat in the Arizona State Legislature, but I will neither block nor interfere with her filing for candidacy out of respect for her conscience." [4]

The decision made, Clare announced her candidacy for the Arizona House of Representatives in June 1974, making clear how her religious commitment 19 years before had led her to this moment: "I vowed my life, my energy, talents and time to teach, to heal, to care about human dignity….It has become apparent to me that I can better promote human dignity if I could reach that place where human need and human freedom are bartered….I want to go to that legislature and be there, an advocate for human need and human liberation. I want to raise my voice in the public forum in defense of the citizen and against those who exploit and manipulate the people. I want to go to Phoenix to struggle for social justice."

Clare already had a credible history of political activity. With degrees in history and political science, she had studied at the Taft Institute of Government at the University of Arizona, and attended two sessions of the Network Legislative Seminar in Washington D.C. A teacher of government and history at Villa Carondelet and Salpointe High School in Tucson, she had participated actively in political and ecumenical groups and social outreach organizations focused on peace, equal rights, farm labor, and the poor. Perhaps her greatest asset was her friend and co-worker Sr. Judith Lovchik.

Clare Dunn, State Representative, District 13, Arizona

An educator by training and profession, Sr. Judy had taught in elementary and secondary schools, served as administrator of Villa Carondelet (formerly St. Joseph's Academy) in Tucson, and as CSJ community supervisor of secondary education.

Clare and Judy ran a vigorous campaign with the enthusiastic support of a large number of CSJs. "Her campaigning efforts, both for others and for herself, put many of us to shame. If there's a door in District 13 that was never knocked on by

Judy and Clare with Bruce Babbitt, Governor of the State of Arizona

Clare Dunn, it must have been installed Friday or yesterday. She hit most of the doors in the district half a dozen times or more." [5]

In November, Clare went to Phoenix representing District 13 in the House of Representatives, with Judy as her legislative assistant. "From her first day in the Legislature, she established herself as a hard worker who did her homework and knew what was happening. She understood the problems of women, minority groups, the poor, the elderly and the handicapped. She fought for legislation to solve some of those problems." [6] Working out of their mutual vision, Judy provided the words, Clare gave them life on the floor. Their partnership became legendary in Phoenix. "Sr. Judith provided some of the power behind the throne. She did the research and wrote speeches for Sr. Clare. Any time you got into a debate with Sr. Clare, you knew you were doing battle with two people. They worked very well together. Sr. Judith was the 61st member of the Legislature." [7]

Clare and Judy served in the Arizona Legislature for over six years, a time of intensive work. They had few victories, many defeats, and ongoing learning about how the political system worked, and how it did not work for the powerless. Their victories were in helping others, not in getting legislation passed. Clare used her skills as a teacher to help others access the system for themselves in order to get legislation for the disabled and the elderly. "Struggle and defeat can burn people out. For Judy and Clare they were a source of strength. As they faced these enemies, they again and again went back to Scripture, especially the Psalms, for inspiration, for courage, for renewal."[8] One of Clare's colleagues in the Legislature commented that "I sensed sometimes that Sr. Clare felt very depressed and I noted that at that time she sought comfort in the Bible. I would be walking by her office and I would see her reading the Psalms."[9]

As Judy and Clare were companions in their ministry and their community life, so they were together at their death. Returning home on July 30, 1981 from a few days vacation at a friend's house in the White mountains, they died tragically in a head-on collision on the I-10. Ironically, the accident was almost in the shadow of Picacho Peak, which had played a threatening role for the original sisters traveling to Tucson in May 1870. The shock of the violence of their deaths, and the tragic loss to their sisters and families and to their ministry to the poor and powerless, were intensified by the irony of the circumstances of the accident. The driver of a truck crowded with immigrant farmworkers had become confused and was traveling the wrong way on the freeway. As cars veered to avoid the oncoming truck, the sisters did not have time to avoid the crash. The two sisters died instantly; the farmworkers, for whom Clare had so much compassion, fled uninjured into the fields.

At the funeral two plain coffins were draped with Mexican serapes. Tucson's St. Augustine's Cathedral was crowded with sisters of St. Joseph, friends and family, representatives of other religious groups, church and city and state officials including the governor, Clare and Judy's constituents and their colleagues at Arizona's House of Representatives. Among the many tributes to the two sisters was this simple statement—"We have lost the conscience of the House."

While CSJs were working with grapepickers in central California, and Sr. Clare was in her first term in the Arizona Legislature, St. Joseph Center began in 1976 with a field trip in Venice, California.

Sr. Marilyn Rudy, teaching social justice at St. Bernard's High School, decided to take her students to see firsthand the lives of the poor not far from their own homes. Deciding she could do something about the poverty she observed on the streets of Venice, Sr. Marilyn was soon joined by Sr. Louise Bernstein with her bilingual skills and her passion for the poor. Together, they founded St. Joseph's Center.

Founders of St. Joseph Center, Sisters Marilyn Rudy and Louise Bernstein

First of all, they needed a place, just a storefront would do. Marilyn canvassed the streets of Venice, looking first for a laundromat which would have a captive audience, rejected a few as too expensive, and finally found the Cinderella Thrift Shop on the corner of Dimmick and Rose. The Cinderella was going out of business, and the owners were happy to rent one room to the sisters at a reasonable rate. Beginning with giving out food and clothes and supported by seed money from the Sisters of St. Joseph, Marilyn and Louise began to put together their goals for the service.

An immediate need was to provide emergency services to low-income families, the elderly, and the homeless. But essential to their vision was empowerment. They wanted to create a safe place where people could be welcomed with respect and concern, treated with dignity, and where they could begin to assume control of their own lives. In a bulletin written during the first year, they described St. Joseph's as "a drop-in center where people can learn about their rights, understand how to improve their nutrition and, most important, a place where they can help themselves to be active, productive members of the Venice community." Another important goal was to serve as a bridge between people in need and those who care about providing assistance. The Center began with the two sisters (one fulltime) and eight student volunteers from St. Bernard's, Loyola-Marymount University, and Mount St. Mary's College.

The Center expanded rapidly from the first two programs. Among additional services, the bulletin that first year lists shelter, employment information, transportation, medical information, legal referrals, and tutoring. Marilyn and Louise found help coming from many places. They began networking through religious groups, local agencies and the business community. Food and clothing donations came from neighboring churches of all denominations. "We couldn't have grown without volunteers, unselfish, dedicated people who believed in the same values Marilyn and I did. They came from the community, from the Sisters of St. Joseph, from neighboring congregations, and of course from the Jesuit Volunteers." [10]

A day center was established in a former laundromat where the homeless could rest and be safe, take a shower, wash their clothes, receive their mail and have access to a telephone. Counseling, referrals to other services, help with job applications, and other

St. Joseph Center rummage sale

social services became available as the center grew. A thrift shop began with a series of rummage sales in school yards and parking lots—"backbreaking hard work, but we met a lot of great people—high school kids, parents, our own sisters of St. Joseph and members of the Venice community. I learned a lot about selling (Marilyn came from a retailing background so we had a little edge)—and junk!" [11] Rummage sales grew into a thrift shop in a small store on Rose Avenue. It kept on growing, always a good source of income, and eventually moved into a good location on Lincoln Boulevard in Santa Monica. Many other spinoffs developed: job-placement, a free child care cooperative, senior outreach, a monetary advisory program.

Probably the most attractive and popular venture was Bread and Roses, a restaurant that had started with another effort to reach out to the poor, making sandwiches to give to the homeless on the beach. The project grew and became a restaurant in a rented building on

Served by the founder at Bread and Roses

Rose Avenue, taking on a character that mirrored the goals of St. Joseph's Center. Bread and Roses Café provides a personal and dignified atmosphere for over one hundred persons served daily—"bread for the nourishment we all need for our bodies...roses for the beauty and graciousness and love which nourish our spirit." [12] Homeless guests make reservations for their meal and are served at tables with tablecloths and flowers, with classical music or jazz in the background. Signing up for reservations helps the chef to plan, but it helps the clients as well. Chef Thomasine Howlett pointed out that "it gives people a sense of responsibility, knowing that if they want to eat that day, they need to check in at the service center and get their name on the list." [13]

St. Joseph chefs Sisters Eileen Mitchell and Rose Cecilia Harrington

As with the other projects, volunteers are important to the functioning of Bread and Roses, helping with food preparation and serving the guests at their tables. Celebrity volunteers mingle with the others. The Los Angeles Clippers basketball team have been frequent volunteers, and a familiar presence at the café has been actor and activist Martin Sheen who became a good friend of Sr. Rose Cecilia Harrington, chief chef for many years. A natural outgrowth of "feeding the poor" at Bread and Roses is the Food Service Training Program, preparing many to work in food services.

In December 1986, St. Joseph's Center became the first CSJ ministry, other than education or health care institutions, to become a sponsored corporation of the Sisters of St. Joseph of Carondelet.

CSJs represent the community on the Board of Directors and minister at St. Joseph's Center in a multitude of ways, but the leadership is increasingly carried out by dedicated laypersons who share the mission and vision of the founders. With the cooperation of the Los Angeles Archdiocese, St. Clement's Parish, and the city of Santa Monica, a new facility was completed in September 2008 on Hampton Drive in Venice housing St. Joseph Center and St. Clement's Pastoral Center.

When Delfia Ramos first came to St. Joseph Center, she didn't know her life was going to turn around. The Center was just getting started, and she was pregnant with her fourth child. Her husband worked, but what he earned was not enough for the family. She needed food and clothing for the children. As a frequent and welcome visitor to the Center, she wanted to give back what she was given and began to volunteer. She bagged food, sorted clothes, and worked at the thrift shop, wherever she could help. As time went by, she began to balance being a wife and mother with working on the staff. For over 25 years until she retired, Delfia was a dedicated staff member at St. Joseph's Family Center. And she is just one of the many success stories told at St. Joseph Center.

CHAPTER 11

LISTENING TO THE CRY OF THE POOR

"In the end, our bonds of unity and reconciliation kept us together."

Barbara Sullivan CSJ

As the 1970s moved into the 1980s, more new ministries started up throughout the province. Among the earliest was the House of Ruth, founded in 1978 in Boyle Heights as a transitional shelter for homeless women and children. Some were battered women who had escaped their homes without papers, clothes, or money; others had been abandoned by their husbands or families. Some were teenage dropouts with babies. Four CSJs—Sisters Judy Molosky, Georgeann O'Brien, Linda Pearson, and Jeanette Van Vleck— lived in community in an old house with these rejected women who needed immediate shelter and a little time to try to establish themselves for a new life. At the beginning, the House of Ruth was supported only by the sisters' stipends and charitable gifts. Currently self-incorporated and no longer staffed by CSJs, the House of Ruth continues to carry CSJ history and mission.

Meanwhile, the Sisters of St. Joseph were trying to define for themselves how their ministry was changing. Their founders' mission was unchanged; the charism still directed them to service of the dear neighbor. But as they listened to the cry of the poor, they were struggling to define who were the poor. Even with the reduced number of what they called CSJ schools, they were still teachers and educators, they still served health care needs in the province. How were they to understand this great shift to new forms of service? What would happen to our schools and our hospitals? What will happen to us?

In the words of a sister in leadership at the time, "We recognized that our boundaries were cracking."[1] It was time to talk and plan together. This also meant trying to surface the pain and anger that went with institutional change. The Provincial Council decided to begin a process of strategic planning, and on September 3, 1982, Sr. Kathleen Mary McCarthy, provincial superior, sent a letter to the sisters of the province announcing that Colarelli Associates, Inc. had been engaged to guide the process in the province.

The first phase of the planning involved the sisters in identifying a contemporary expression of their enduring mission. Five elements of the expression emerged: focus on mission, response to needs in geographic areas, collaboration, multi-level networking, and ongoing planning. The thinking began to shift away from a focus on structures—schools and hospitals—and more toward response to perceived needs. Structure would follow to support response.

In the last phase of the planning, the sisters entered into an intense discussion of five possible models of service the province could follow. One model was to halt the planning to focus on re-examination of the meaning of mission, the second was to decrease the number of ministerial commitments in order to concentrate sister resources, the third was to restructure ministries to facilitate partnership with the laity, the fourth was to disengage from all commitments and convert assets to endowment funds to free sisters for mission. To the surprise of many involved in the process, the province voted almost unanimously for the fifth option—to decentralize structures, and to network and expand ministries through partnership in mission with the laity.

By August 1983, a province vision was being drafted. It read in part: *"To be mission focused will require us to focus on our commitment to persons and their needs rather than on specific forms of ministry. We have always served people and will continue to do so, but our ministries will be determined by the needs of those people to whom we are committed. This means our ministries will change as the needs of those to whom we are committed change. It means our ministries will be flexible, always open to both the tried and new ways of organizing resources to respond to needs. Our committed presence will continually call for the adaptation of ministries to meet changing needs, and a response that will accomplish our commitment to reconcile each person with self, with others, with the world, and with God."*

Slowly, still painfully, ways of managing ministry began to change. Regional superiors talked with pastors and bishops to explain that the community could no longer guarantee to provide CSJ principals and staff for their schools. Although sisters continued to teach in many of the formerly "CSJ schools", the community moved to a more independent position, undertaking to provide sisters' cars and to pay rent for the convents.

A significant change happened behind the scenes with the process of missioning. Sisters were no longer missioned to local communities where they would work, but rather to their specific ministry. The old missioning board with slots for every local community disappeared. In the end, ways of supporting the CSJ mission became more clear, trust grew—and healing. Sisters were learning to talk with each other about things that affected their lives and the future of the community.

Meanwhile, while the careful process of reorganizing ministry service was moving along, new ministries were growing rapidly. Sisters Joanna Bramble and Pat Sears had started to do community organizing in West Oakland as early as 1973, opening a community services center in a public housing project. As their work expanded, they saw the critical need for housing in the neighborhood they served and, inspired by a visit to Jubilee Housing in Washington D.C., they

Jubilee West founders Sisters Pat Sears and Joanna Bramble. Los Angeles Times Photo

established their own West Oakland housing project in 1980 naming it Jubilee West. Although they knew nothing about real estate and had no money, they began to buy and fix up abandoned houses to make them affordable to poverty-level families. The project quickly grew with its mission to provide decent and safe housing, to expand community services and youth programs, and to empower people of the neighborhood to enrich the quality of their lives. Living in a shelter was much better than being on the streets, said a single mother of four. But when you are in a shelter, you are still homeless, and being homeless is belittling. Now she loves it when people ask for her address.

For many years, Jubilee West continued to expand housing for low-rent occupancy while offering programs for single mothers and children including parenting skills, health education, literacy, English as a Second Language, and training in job search and interviewing. Empowerment was the key—providing tools whereby people choose to empower themselves in controlling their own lives. Pat and Joanna carried on a tradition of service begun over a hundred years ago in Oakland by sisters of St. Joseph until 1993, when Jubilee West housing was transferred to the East Bay Asian Development Corporation. Although the intent had been to carry on the original mission, with the elimination of almost all government funding to subsidize housing for poor families, the Jubilee West units are now no longer within reach of the poor. "Often with our best efforts, circumstances beyond our control make our long-term goals impossible." [2]

In 1982, two years after Jubilee West began in West Oakland, Sr. Michele Marie Morris opened a small soup kitchen in Lawndale, California, naming it House of Yahweh. In the beginning, she was able to feed ten to fifteen people every day. With the pressing needs of the poor and homeless in that South Bay area of Los Angeles, the House of Yahweh expanded rapidly into a network of services. Over the years, thousands have been served with warm meals, food boxes, clothing, furniture, temporary housing, and counseling services aimed at enabling people to regain confidence and get back on their feet.

Good Shepherd Center began with a sister of St. Joseph dressed in her traditional black habit walking the streets of Skid Row, searching for lost, abandoned and runaway teenagers. Sr. Julia Mary Farley was working in the Angels' Flight program of the Los Angeles Catholic Welfare Bureau when she extended her ministry to the countless broken, homeless women she found in the streets and parks. She did what she could to minister to them there on the streets, and soon a drop-in shelter took shape. In 1984, with the encouragement of Cardinal Timothy Manning, Good Shepherd Center began as a program of Catholic Charities, and Sr. Julia Mary started her long tenure as director of the center.

Located at first in the former Our Lady of Loretto convent as an emergency shelter, Good Shepherd rapidly expanded to other locations and ministries. Perhaps the most impressive is their outreach program—a sister and an assistant in a van combing the areas of MacArthur and Lafayette parks searching out women and children desperately in need and not knowing where to reach out for help. Living in doorways, public restrooms, train stations and under freeways, many are hopeless and distrustful of offers of assistance. The van always goes supplied with coffee

Sr. Julia Mary Farley, founder of Good Shepherd Center, receives an award for her dedication to the poor.

and sandwiches, doughnuts and hard-boiled eggs, and there is always an offer of a safe place to stay. Sometimes it takes months to gain their trust so they will make a first visit to Good Shepherd. Some women never come and have to be left behind in their dark lives. In every stop of the outreach van and in every Good Shepherd program, women and children are offered, with respect and love, the opportunity to remake their lives with hope.[3]

As sisters were creating ministries, they found they were also entering the world of business. They needed seed money for start-up, advice and backing from people experienced in this kind of work, and legal coverage. In April 1986, the Los Angeles Province Assembly asked that a corporation be initiated which could sponsor beginning projects until they could stand on their own. This idea grew into the Sisters of St. Joseph Ministerial Services which began in 1989 as a non-profit corporate structure to house new ministries until they could be separately incorporated. Fledgling ministries enjoyed financial and technical assistance and necessary legal protection from liability issues. With this new province service, networking and collaboration with lay people became important components. The mission statement described Ministerial Services as a partnership of people who recognize the value of the mission of the sisters and seek to make a difference in the lives of those in need. Lay people and CSJ Associates have traditionally served with the sisters on the Board of Directors.

Many creative ministries began and flourished through Ministerial Services. Some fulfilled their goals and closed after a few years. Others started with the help of Ministerial Services and eventually became independent, obtaining their own corporate status. St. Joseph's Center is the unique example of a ministry which began through Ministerial Services, obtained its corporate identity, and then requested to be sponsored by the Sisters of St. Joseph. A few works, including Making the Right Connections and El Centrito De La Colonia, were founded by lay people in collaboration with CSJs. Currently, two emerging ministries are under the SSJMS umbrella—Restorative Partners in San Luis Obispo and St. Joseph Worker, a congregation-wide ministry.

In these years of high activity, some sisters found opportunities in ministries already established. Sr. Kathy Stein served as program director at Thomas House, a free shelter enabling families to stay together up to six months receiving classes in English, assistance in job search and training, budgeting and nutrition while they work to become independent. In Sr. Ines Telles's work with high-risk youth in the Soledad Enrichment Action program in East Los Angeles, she saw that young gang members are not likely to change unless their

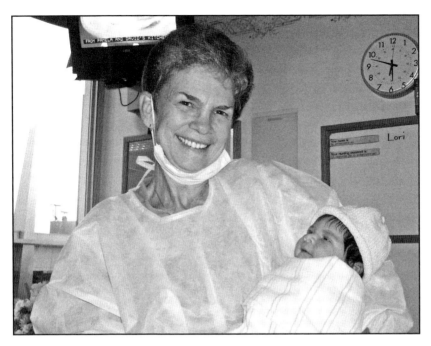

Sr. Kathy Stein, longtime director of Thomas House, welcomes a new member to the community.

homes change as well. "We can't get better until our parents change." So she developed a curriculum in parenting—*Breaking the Circle of Domestic Violence*. A longtime educator in her many years as a missionary in Peru, Sister Ines took another step and trained parents to teach the program, *Parents Helping Parents*.[4]

On September 15, 1996, a new addition to the Ministerial Services Corporation opened its doors in mid-city Los Angeles. With special support as well from the Immaculate Heart community, Alexandria House offers hospitality and temporary residence to women and children in need. The neighborhood benefits as well. In their desire to build community, the staff welcomes women of the neighborhood to share in their educational services and technical assistance, as well as in services like afterschool tutoring. Sr. Judy Vaughan, founder of Alexandria House, was honored as a Woman of Justice in 1997 by NETWORK, national Catholic social justice organization.

In 1990, three sisters started yet another service to the poor and destitute in Oakland. Sisters Carol Anne O'Marie, Maureen Lyons, and Suzanne Steffen opened A Friendly Place, a drop-in center for homeless women. Five years later, they were able to purchase a larger building—A Friendly Manor—which added temporary and permanent housing for their guests. Reflecting on the outpouring of support from the sisters and the surrounding community (many of

Founders of A Friendly Place, Sisters Carol Anne O'Marie and Maureen Lyons, announce a new residential service.

whom were taught by Sisters of St. Joseph), Sr. Carol Anne remembered the CSJ saying—where one of us is, we all are. In all of our works, she pointed out, whether teaching children, healing the sick, or extending welcome to the homeless, we all work for the poor. "It has given me courage and a great sense of pride to be a member of our congregation where together we can do more in one day than any one of us could do in several lifetimes."

With the proliferation of their ministries to the poor during the years following the second Vatican Council, the sisters were following the original call of their founder to divide the city, to seek out and address the needs of God's people. *Design for Renewal* had urged them "to teach, to help the sick and needy, to be a sacrament of His mercy in the world." As they continued the traditional ministries and started new ones, they were also intensifying their work for justice in the world.

The province justice office has played a significant role in justice actions over the years. Working with Province Assembly, staff have developed policies on social responsibility for province investments and provided education on issues like immigration, health care, racism, gun control, euthanasia, and human trafficking. In 1989 the office developed processes of theological reflection for addressing non-violence.

Sisters have been involved with justice on many levels. CSJs have been sponsored by the province to work with the economically poor. Others have done public witness against nuclear warfare at the Nevada test site, joined protests of the School of the Americas at Fort Benning, Georgia, offered hospitality to Central American refugees, and joined in boycotts and acts of civil disobedience, sometimes ending in arrests. Countless sisters participate in justice actions

Sisters Catherine Marie Kreta and Veronica Miracle held regular protests on Sunset Boulevard.

through prayer, vigils, letter-writing, phone calls, and recycling. Supporting the public statement of the province against human trafficking, sisters—including retired sisters in wheelchairs—regularly appear on Sunset Boulevard with their banners protesting this modern day slavery.

The post-Vatican II years were also a time of individual spiritual deepening. Following the direction of the Second Vatican Council, *Design for Renewal* encouraged the sisters to take more responsibility for personal growth in prayer and spirituality, and for development of their own gifts. Spiritual direction became an important part of many sisters' spirituality, and a new ministry as well. The Los Angeles Archdiocesan Spirituality Center, begun in 1983 by Sr. Thomas Bernard MacConnell, offers a three-year program in spiritual direction. Still in existence as the Spirituality Center and housed on Mount St. Mary's Doheny campus, the Center serves as a place of information, direction and support for those desiring to grow in their relationship with God. Encouraged to make thirty-day retreats and sabbaticals, and to develop new contemplative prayer styles, the Sisters of St. Joseph increasingly are identifying themselves as contemplatives in action.

A contemplative spirit flows easily into an appreciation of one's own gifts in an atmosphere of creative leisure. Sr. Monica Miller, artist and teacher, was beloved by many for her gentle way of treating children with love and reverence, and turning materials into things of beauty. Her dreams of pursuing a formal career in art put aside because her eyesight had been damaged by smallpox in childhood, she turned to working with ceramics. "I could use my hands more easily than my eyes in this medium." Her "Monique" statues of the Blessed Virgin and the Holy Family are still treasured in the community. Encouraging sisters to explore their creative gifts, the province Committee on the Arts displayed design, painting, photography and crafts, and helped to provide opportunities to attend theater, opera, symphonies, and museums. Book clubs of all kinds flourish. Carondelet Productions was founded in 1992 to support and affirm the arts ministries of sisters and CSJ Associate artists. Currently under the title of Carondelet Artists, the organization encourages and assists CSJ artists to develop and market their work and maintains the Carondelet Center gift shop.

CSJs have always been an articulate group, and good writing has been a way of life for many. The early history of Mount St. Mary's College was preserved by Sr. Dolorosa Mannix in her colorful reminiscences; Sr. St. Claire Coyne researched and wrote the history of the western province as part of the history of the Sisters of St. Joseph of Carondelet, published in 1966. Sr. Laurentia Digges, professor of English at the college, received the national first prize from the Thomas More Association in 1957 for *Transfigured World*. This study of the relationship of the liturgy to the world about us was followed by *Adam's Haunted Sons*, also selected as a Thomas More Book Club selection. With all her years teaching Bible as Literature at the Mount, she had never found a good textbook for the course. So she wrote her own, exploring as a literary critic the human experience behind the familiar biblical stories. Good teaching was always central to the Mount's drive to excellence. Alumnae credit Sr. Laurentia and the other English faculty with the dozens of national student awards for creative writing.

CSJs have published as journalists and historians; they have received recognition for their scholarly work, poetry, essays and articles. Sisters write in province publications—*Designs, Futures* and, more recently, *CSJ*—about the life, thought, and prayer of the province. Sr. Carol Anne O'Marie was certainly the most prolific writer of fiction with her Sister Mary Helen series of detective novels. Her last novel, *Like a Swarm of Bees*, published posthumously, recreated the first pioneer years of the Sisters of St. Joseph in Carondelet, Missouri, told through the eyes of the youngest member of the group, Sr. St. Protais Deboille.

Moving into partial retirement does not put an end to ministry for most sisters who find their good work can go right on with shorter hours and limited responsibilities. Many CSJs are still working in the field of education, but now as tutors, teacher aides, and advisors. Health care ministry now includes partially retired sisters working as pastoral visitors and volunteers. CSJs serve as board members in all areas of ministry, and bring CSJ presence, mission and spirituality wherever they continue to minister.

In the later years of retirement, Prayer and Witness becomes ministry for the elderly sisters. Holy Family Community was established in 1979 in the north wing of Carondelet Center, a significant change for the building which began in 1955 as a House of Studies for the young sisters. Planning for a retirement home had started as early as 1971. St. Mary's Hospital in Tucson was being phased out as a retirement residence, and Daniel Freeman Hospital convent could no longer accommodate the growing numbers of retired. After several locations were considered and rejected, the decision was made to redesign the original novitiate classrooms and 26 dormitories at Carondelet Center to create a retirement community, designed for sick and frail sisters in need of medical or supportive care. In Holy Family's first year, there were 709 sisters in the western province, 95 over the age of 70. The average age of sisters in the province was 50.

The chapel for Holy Family Community, established in 1979

In September 1979, Sr. Thomas Bernard MacConnell, first superior of the community, along with about 20 sisters, took up residence in the renovated north wing and Holy Family Community

Sr. Roberta Warren, life of the party at Holy Family

began. Always central to the vision of the retirement center was that it was a local community, a home for the sisters who lived there. A constant norm was to avoid institutional atmosphere whenever possible. Staff were told that "Carondelet Center is home for the sisters in Holy Family Community. As we provide specific care, we encourage all staff to constantly keep in mind that they enter our home to assist the sisters with their specific needs. We are a home which provides home nursing rather than a nursing home."

As the years have passed, the understanding of religious life has changed. By the time Sr. Sharon Margaret Ninteman joined the staff in 1999, she was appointed as coordinator of community life, rather than local superior. The constant effort has been to maintain a sense of home, allowing the sisters to live religious life together, caring for themselves as much as possible, staying informed, sharing in community decisions, making personal choices. The regional superior keeps her door wide open, and maintains a religious presence on the administrative team. Ministry continues for everyone—one is a ward clerk at the nursing desk, another keeps the finances straight for the community, many make phone calls and write letters for justice issues. They minister to each other when they can, delivering mail and snacks, reading to each other, pushing wheelchairs, sitting with their sisters listening or in quiet prayer.

In June 2012, there were 340 sisters in the Los Angeles Province, 267 over 70 years old. The average age was 76. Holy Family has now come near to reaching full capacity and in a few years the numbers will start to decrease. Soon it will be time to begin to plan again for the best usage of Carondelet Center. Meanwhile, the ministry of prayer and presence continues.

CHAPTER 12

Behold, I am making something new

As the century began, the life of the province changed noticeably. Ministries were as vital as ever, the sisters seemed even busier, but they were beginning to ask new questions. Numbers were declining, the sisters were aging, but ministry and province government seemed to become increasingly complex. It was a time for evaluation. The years of the new millennium took on a thoughtful tone, a time to be contemplative and listen to the Spirit. It became a time of wisdom.

But contemplation did not mean sitting still. Sisters of St. Joseph were still heavily involved in ministry and justice activity. Forms of province government claimed more and more time. Most sisters met regularly with their clusters for prayer, the CSJ practice of Sharing of the Heart, and intense discussion and voting on proposals. Province Assembly brought everyone together once a year for three days of province business. The 2012 Province Chapter broke ground, becoming open to all qualified sisters who wished to participate. The many forms of technology transformed the conversation of the province, linking friends and groups and committees. And, of course, added to the work.

Change was the keynote during these first years of the new century. Committees and clusters pondered how to restructure province and congregational government to fit decreasing numbers and changing needs. Questions were asked. Are there more effective ways to encourage new membership? Out of this came the House of Discernment with CSJs living in community with women reflecting on their vocation call. How can we best communicate with each other and with others beyond the province? New forms of publication blossomed. The monthly *Designs* was supplemented with a weekly *e-designs*. The reflective look at a single theme in *CSJ* replaced *Futures*. Connections formed easily with all parts of the congregation and other religious groups. The sisters in Japan brought a great gift of new life when they joined the Los Angeles province as a region.

The Japanese vice-province becomes a region of Los Angeles province. Row one from left Sisters Anne Michael Kuwabara, Francesca Inoue, Grace Marie Saito, Barbara Anne Stowasser, Lucia Yamada, Mary Nicholas Inoue. Second row from left Sisters Christina Takeichi, Mary Veronica Murata, Madeline Marie Nakatsu, Mary Paul Morimoto, Barbara Mary Sanborn, Theresa Kvale. Top row from left Sisters Serena Baba, Laura Bufano, Miriam Maki, Maria Teresa Mitani.

Into this reflective and changing world came the shock of a sudden announcement from the Vatican in December 2008. The Congregation for Institutes of Consecrated Life had initiated an apostolic visitation of women religious in the United States. This action was followed the next April with another announcement, this time from the Congregation of the Doctrine of the Faith. The Leadership Conference of Women Religious would be undergoing a doctrinal investigation. This double investigation into the treasured life and mission of women religious was to absorb thought and energy of American congregations for many months.

Dismay and hurt were soon followed by a determination to respond to the challenges by communicating an accurate picture of contemporary religious life not only in America but worldwide. The western province worked closely with the rest of the congregation in responding to the investigations, and soon collaboration spread to other American congregations, and ultimately worldwide. With all the pain of these challenges from the Church, women religious came to renewed self-definition and a stronger confidence in their mission. It was definitely a time of growth.

The spirit of collaboration had been an essential part of the congregation's history from its founding. Lay women were part of the first group whom Father Medaille brought together in Le Puy in the middle of the 17th century. Sisters of St. Joseph and lay women ministered together to the poor and prisoners there in southern France. The early documents even show that the first novice director for the little group was Marguerite de St.-Laurent, a lay woman. So when the second Vatican Council encouraged the role of the laity in the Church, planning for a more formal inclusion of lay people in the mission of the Sisters of St. Joseph was a natural development. Lay association evolved throughout the 1970s, and in 1978 the General Chapter adopted the statement that "Each province may make provision for lay associates who share the charism of the Sisters of St. Joseph but do not intend to make profession in the Congregation."

The Los Angeles province began planning its associate program in 1980 with two principles in mind. "First, let it evolve from the actual experience of the people and the sisters interested in developing it. Second, assure that the finalized version after the 'lived experience phase' is a collaborative effort of both associates and sisters."[1] For the next three years, a planning board composed of Sisters Rita Angerman, Rose Cecilia Harrington, Eileen Mitchell, and Marceline Vidovich, together with an equal number of potential associates, developed a rich program of experiences enabling both associates and CSJs to get acquainted with the concept of association and to share the spirituality and traditions of the community. Early enrichment days focused on call and vocation, ministry, charism and reconciliation. Gradually, future associates were integrated into province events and liturgies.

In November 1983, the CSJ Associate program was approved by the Provincial Council, and on September 29, 1984, the founding group of CSJ Associates made their commitments in a formal ceremony in Carondelet Center chapel. The first group included Esther Angerman, Teri Bastian, Mary Lou Donohue, Patricia Hart, Mary Ann Healy, Eileen McDonald, and Leonard Stevling. It was a diverse group including men and women; four had served on the planning board, three were parents of a CSJ, and one was a former Sister of St. Joseph.

CSJ Associate pioneers. Seated from left Sr. Marceline Vidovich, Leonard Stevling, Eleanor Angerman, Mary Lou Donohue. Standing from left Sr. Eileen Mitchell, Pat Hart, Teri Bastian, Sr. Rose Cecilia Harrington, Sr. Rita Angerman, Mary Ann Healy

Once established, the associate movement spread to all parts of the province—Arizona and the Pacific Northwest, the San Francisco Bay area, San Diego, and all parts of Los Angeles. Associates now serve on province boards and committees, and attend CSJ gatherings, clusters, assemblies, and chapters. In many situations they have assumed responsibility in province offices. The program, currently numbering close to 200 associates and candidates, continues to flourish under the leadership of a director and a board composed of associates and sisters.

"Those who began the Associate movement in the Los Angeles province likened their efforts to one of Fr. Medaille's favorite images, the mustard seed of the gospel—the smallest of all seeds, yet imbued with the active grace and presence of the Holy Spirit, becoming a great tree that will provide a home that welcomes diversity." [2] The vision of Fr. Medaille and the first six sisters had become a reality—vowed and non-vowed members committed together to the mission.

Collaboration grew even more important in recent years as numbers decreased. Deliberate planning to share the mission and charism with lay partners led to a creative widening of the tent of membership. The St. Joseph Worker program, a CSJ-supported ministry across the congregation, welcomes young women to make a one-year commitment of volunteer service with the poor and marginated. Sharing the CSJ spirituality, they live simply in small intentional communities. Sr. Judy Molosky directs the program in Los Angeles, placing the women in a variety of sites and mentoring them into leadership for social and spiritual transformation.

With fewer sisters having the ability and energy to take leadership of CSJ-sponsored institutions, lay people became partners in these ministries. By 2012, the college, the high schools, and St. Joseph Center all had lay women and men in top positions. In 2002, Carondelet-sponsored hospitals became part of Ascension Health, a Catholic health system. By 2010 as more congregations joined Ascension, the congregational sponsors recognized that single sponsorship would be more effective for the functioning of the ministry. The next year the Vatican approved creation of a non-congregational public juridic person to serve as sole sponsor of Ascension Health. Through Sponsorship of the Whole, all the sponsors steward, as one, the combined overall health ministry. In a relationship of mutuality and communion the sponsors work together to continue and strengthen the healing ministry of Jesus.

Throughout this process of stepping back from direct control of their institutions, sisters found themselves living the familiar maxim of their founder, Fr. Jean-Pierre Medaille:

"Advance good works till near their completion
and then, if it can be done easily,
let others finish them and gain all the credit."

CSJ ministries are interwoven more than ever with the work and support of lay partners, not only because there is no longer a large work force of sisters, but in recognition that the mission of the Church is the privilege and responsibility of all the baptized.

For many years, Sisters of St. Joseph were known for their service in education and health care. Those areas have broadened in response to the needs of society and the gifts of the sisters. As they open people's minds to urgent justice issues like racism, immigration and human trafficking, they are acting as educators. As they visit prisons and walk with the poor, they are helping to heal and comfort the suffering.

Visiting prisons in the 21st century is a long way from walking the cobbled streets to bring comfort to prisoners in 17th century Le Puy. Now buses make the trip to prisons all over California bringing prisoners' children to visit their mothers and fathers. Get on the Bus began as an outgrowth of Women in Criminal Justice Network, a movement involving religious communities, criminal justice professionals, former prisoners, and concerned citizens. The group focused on issues involving women in prison whose numbers had increased by 500% during the 1990s.

In 1999, Women and Criminal Justice representatives visited the women's prisons in Chowchilla, California—at the time, the largest women's prison complex in the world with over 8000 prisoners. During these visits, representatives spent time listening to prisoners speak about their needs. A collective heartbreak was shared again and again—"We never see our children." Out of this cry for help, Sr. Suzanne Steffen founded Get on the Bus as her volunteer ministry. Three years later, Sr. Suzanne Jabro took on leadership of the organization and its web of grassroots, faith-based volunteers. The Sisters of St. Joseph Ministerial Services sponsored the project in its early years.

Get on the Bus started with one bus, nine families and seventeen children traveling to Valley State Prison for Women in Chowchilla on Mother's Day. Today, dozens of buses bring over a thousand children to ten women's and men's prisons throughout California to spend a few precious hours with their parents. The ministry is shared by CSJs, friends and associates of the sisters, employees of the vast prison system, even by prisoners themselves who raise money to contribute to the expenses of the project.

Get on the Bus brings families together

Get on the Bus has caught the hearts and imaginations of people throughout the world who can empathize with children experiencing the pain, loss and stigma of having a parent in prison. Sr. Suzanne Jabro sees the link of Le Puy with Chowchilla: "These necessary

Sr. Suzanne Jabro

Sisters Teresa Lynch and Irene Najera with the children of St. Genevieve's School

efforts represent a full circle of ministry to the dear neighbor from our founding to the present day. The same Spirit is still calling us to the margins."

In her history of the Los Angeles Province, Sister St. Claire Coyne reflected on the early experience of the first sisters in Arizona who in addition to founding academies, hospitals, Indian schools and an orphanage "were the sole assistants of the few diocesan priests in the territory."[3] More sisters now are taking

Sr. Joyce Marie Gaspardo visits the dear neighbor.

on leadership roles in church ministry. Three CSJs—Sisters Barbara Flannery, Sara Kane, and Cecilia Louise Moore—have served as chancellors in California dioceses. Others nurture the spiritual mission of the church as parish life directors, pastoral associates, directors and teachers of religious education.

The direct ministry of education continues in schools with CSJs serving in classrooms, offices, libraries, computer labs, and board rooms. Carondelet High School added a new position to their staff—that of CSJ mentor to lay administrators. Sisters continue to care

Sr. Callista Roy

In November 2007, the American Academy of Nursing conferred an outstanding honor on Sr. Callista Roy CSJ. She became part of an elite group of "Living Legends," nursing professionals who are extraordinary role models and reminders of the proud history of nursing.

Sr. Callista is known throughout the world for the creation of the Roy Adaptation Model, a nursing theory which defines the individual holistically as an adaptive system with ability to cope in a complex environment. The adaptation model develops the role of the nurse to help patients and their families collaborate as agents of handling health and disease through instruction, education, comfort, and professional care. First implemented by Sr. Callista in the nursing program of Mount St. Mary's College, the Roy model is now part of nursing curricula in many parts of the world and used extensively in nursing practice.

An outpouring of articles and books translated in many languages abundantly documents her contribution to the field of nursing. The model is the basis for over 350 research projects published in English. This CSJ living legend has received honors and awards from all over the world—among them honorary doctorates, a Fulbright Senior Scholar award, filmed interviews, and inaugural addresses. She has a library named for her at Community Health Post in Freetown, Sierra Leone. Perhaps among her favorites is the Carondelet Medal, Mount St. Mary's highest award, conferred in 1995.

Callista started out life as the oldest girl in a family of seven girls and seven boys. Growing up in a loving family and with the encouragement of her mother, a licensed vocational nurse, Callista was drawn to the service profession of nursing. But her first life choice was to a religious vocation. After entering the Sisters of St. Joseph in 1957,

(continued on next page)

she completed a B.A. degree with a nursing major at Mount St. Mary's College. Following nursing ministries in St. Joseph's Hospital in Lewiston, Idaho, and St. Mary's Hospital, Tucson, she earned a master's degree at UCLA in 1964, and soon joined the nursing faculty at the Mount. Encouraged by Sr. Rebecca Doan, chair of the nursing department and founder of the Mount's nursing program, Callista began to develop and implement her adaptation model.

Other study followed—a Ph.D. in sociology from UCLA and a post-doctoral fellowship in Neuroscience Nursing at the University of California at San Francisco. While maintaining her faculty position at Mount St. Mary's and serving for many years as department chair, Callista has served as Adjunct Professor of Nursing at the University of Portland, visiting professor at the University of Conception, Chili, lecturer at the University of San Francisco, Distinguished Visiting Professor at Vanderbilt University, and associate research nurse in the department of neurosurgery at the University of California, San Francisco.

Sr. Callista is currently Professor and Nurse Theorist in the Boston College School of Nursing. Living in faculty housing on the Boston College campus in Chestnut Hill, Massachusetts, she maintains a demanding schedule of teaching, research, and travel all over the world for lectures and conferences. Along with Los Angeles, Boston is home for her. She is so invested in the life of the city that she has received recognition from the Massachusetts House of Representatives for her volunteer work with women in prison. While she is home, Callista prides herself on maintaining a generous "bed and breakfast" for sister visitors to Boston.

for physical, psychological, and spiritual health. Some do direct health care; others are hospital administrators, directors of mission integration, chaplains, pastoral visitors and board members.

When Fr. Medaille gathered the first group of Sisters of St. Joseph, he sent them out into the poorest parts of Le Puy to search out those in need. The term he might have used has come down through the traditions of the congregation—sisters were to go out and "divide the city." Circumstances and cultures change, but history repeats itself. The poor and marginated are still out there longing for help, and in Arizona a sister of St. Joseph gathered her friends and partners to circle the city.

When Sr. Adele O'Sullivan began work as a physician with Health

Care for the Homeless in Phoenix, she saw her ministry as one with the CSJ mission— "to engage in works of compassion and mercy that respond to the spiritual and corporal needs of persons in our times."

Dr. Adele O'Sullivan, founder of Circle the City

As Adele provided health care for the homeless in Phoenix from 1996 to 2009, she experienced firsthand the desperate health needs of the poor and homeless. She began to appeal to the CSJ community and to friends and faith groups in Phoenix for help. Donations, first kept in a shoebox, eventually grew into a bank account, and volunteers gathered. Out of this growing response came Circle the City.

Beginning under the sponsorship of Sisters of St. Joseph Ministerial Services, Circle the City provided health care to the uninsured and counseling to victims of abuse, many of whom had been trafficked. Among other services, it sponsored a housing project, helping parents and their children into safe and permanent housing. As services expanded, an urgent need was recognized. Homeless persons might be fortunate enough to get professional care in a hospital, but when they were discharged, they literally had no place to go. Circle the City set out to establish the first medical respite center in the state of Arizona. Steadily gathering more and more supporters and volunteers, Adele and her board of directors achieved their goal. Circle the City Medical Respite Center opened on September 28, 2012 providing homeless men and women a place to heal with holistic compassionate care. Dedicated professionals and case managers give their patients an opportunity to heal physically, socially, and emotionally, with the hope that many will be able to break the cycle of homelessness.

Of the many awards Sr. Adele has received over the years as a family physician, the most memorable was in April 2008 when she was honored as "One of the Ten Most Caring Persons in America." In her remarks at the presentation in Washington D.C., Adele described herself as a member of the Sisters of St. Joseph, a community with roots in 17th century France when the sisters worked among the street people of that era. "The sisters lived together in community, prayed together and went out into the streets to do what the community was founded to do: love God and love neighbor without distinction." Adele has the privilege of carrying out that heritage with the street people of Phoenix, of knowing the people who live on the streets, in alleys, cars, campsites of every kind, and she compassionately cares for them. [4]

Afterword

As we look at the decreasing numbers of sisters in the congregation, we also look back to our beginnings. Six women gathered in the little French town of Le Puy in the 1650s to commit themselves to a life of service to those whom their founder, Jean Pierre Medaille, called the dear neighbor. Under the patronage of St. Joseph, the community began.

Almost 200 years later, another six came across the Atlantic, arriving by river boat in St. Louis to begin a ministry of service in a new country with new customs and a new language to learn.

Thirty-four years later, seven young sisters of St. Joseph traveled across a desert to what must have seemed to them a new world. They were facing all things new—a rough frontier town, houses made of mud and straw, desert heat, sandy winds, and new ways of living. Five of them, recently from France, had to learn English, Spanish, and the Indian languages spoken in the west.

Our history has a pattern of starting small and growing under God's hand to meet the needs of the neighbor.

"The last CSJ has not yet been born." These words of Sr. Mary Kevin Ford, superior general in the 1970s, linger with us. What this CSJ will be and look like, and what language she will speak, we do not know. But we do know, in the words of one of our leaders, "that we are passing along our charism to those who can sustain it." [1]

A New Harvest

They had learned
the total emptying of self
to be filled with God,
these black-robed women
who carried their baskets to the poor,
bathed the sick,
gently tended the wounded,
and lovingly gathered together
the orphans in their outstretched arms.

Uncommon women
for an uncommon time,
they were not formed by formal rules
to be the congregation
of the great love of God.

The world still needs
their kind of loving.
With a new harvest
the chaff is scattered by the wind.

Through different pathways
women will come
with new voices taking up the singing.
They will come and listen
to the unspoken,
walk in strange places,
and dream strong dreams.

Alberta Cammack, CSJ

Provincial Leadership
Los Angeles Province

May 7, 1876   Western Province established

1876 – 1877   Mother Irene Facemaz

1877 – 1881   Mother Mary Basil Morris

1881 – 1890   Mother Gonzaga Grand

1890 – 1900   Western Province discontinued, Arizona and California becoming part of St. Louis Province. 1899 General Chapter reinstated the Western Province with mandate to change the location. Provincialate established at St. Mary's Academy, Los Angeles, May 1, 1903.

1900 - 1906   Mother Mary Elizabeth Parrot

1906 – 1912   Mother Herman Joseph O'Gorman

1912 - 1916   Mother Mary Marcella Manifold

1917 – 1923   Mother St. Catherine Beavers

1923 – 1929   Mother Margaret Mary Brady

1929 – 1935   Mother Mary Elesia Dwyer

1935 – 1941   Mother Mary Killian Corbett

1941 – 1947   Mother Mary William Flanagan

1947 – 1953   Mother Rosemary Lyons

1953 – 1959   Mother Mary Rosaleen Lynch

1959 – 1965   Mother Mary Josephine Feeley

1965 – 1968   Mother Agnes Marie O'Loughlin

1968 – 1974   Sr. Mary Brigid Fitzpatrick

1974 – 1980	Sr. Grace Ann Loperena
1980 – 1986	Sr. Kathleen Mary McCarthy
1986 – 1992	Sr. Catherine Marie Kreta

Beginning in 1992, provincials were appointed with two assistants with the expectation that the three would function as a team.

1992 – 1998	Sr. Joyce Marie Gaspardo, Sr. Cecilia Louise Moore, Sr. Maureen O'Connor
1998 – 2001	Sr. Maureen O'Connor, Sr. Kathleen Kelly, Sr. Claire Marie Williams
2001 – 2004	Sr. Maureen O'Connor, Sr. Kathleen Kelly, Sr. Ann Patricia O'Connor
2004 – 2010	Sr. Mary McKay, Sr. Patricia Ann Nelson, Sr. Mary Sevilla
2010 -	Sr. Barbara Anne Stowasser, Sr. Theresa Kvale, Sr. Sandra Williams

Notes

CHAPTER 1
1. St. Louis archives
2. St. Louis archives
3. Cammack, "Sister Monica Corrigan"
4. Quotations in the rest of the chapter taken from *Trek of the Seven Sisters*
5. In a postscript to her diary Sister Monica adds: "The bishop was never able to find out who had given the order for the soldiers to meet the sisters. All that the commandant at the fort could tell was that a very respectable, hasty messenger arrived at the fort with the request that a detachment be sent immediately to escort some travelers through the dangerous passes." (Coyne, 293)
6. St. Louis archives

CHAPTER 2
1. McMahon, 62
2. Archives. Hereafter, this will designate the Los Angeles archives.
3. Corrigan, *Arizona—Missioners*
4. The initials CSJ are the approved designation for a Sister of St. Joseph of Carondelet.
5. Sprouffske, "Western Province"
6. Cammack, "Florence, Arizona"
7. Cammack
8. Coyne, 355
9. Cammack, "St. Joseph's Orphan Home"
10. Coyne, 323
11. Savage, *Century's Harvest*, 224

CHAPTER 3
1. Letters and recollections from the sisters are in the Los Angeles archives.
2. McMahon, 83
3. Coyne, 339
4. McMahon, 88
5. Benton, 1
6. Quinn
7. McNeil, "St. Anthony's Indian School", 4
8. McNeil, 5
9. McNeil, 7
10. Benton, 6
11. Cammack, "Mission San Xavier"
12. McMahon, 76

13. McMahon, 78
14. Savage, *The Congregation*, 293
15. Coyne, 343

CHAPTER 4
1. Coyne, 298
2. Coyne
3. Archives
4. Archives
5. Savage, *The Congregation*, 267
6. Fleck
7. Fields
8. Fields
9. Fields
10. Sprouffske, "St. Joseph Institute"
11. Sprouffske
12. Smith, 67
13. Smith, 72
14. Smith, 73
15. Sr. M. Adrienne Kennedy, unpublished notes

CHAPTER 5
1. One of the visitors at this time was Mother Seraphine Ireland, superior of the Carondelet St. Paul province, who studied the situation but was unable to send sisters. A quarter of a century later, the St. Paul province did send sisters to support the ministries when the Lewiston sisters joined the Carondelets.
2. "It was not uncommon at the time for sisters to move freely in or out of other diocesan communities because they knew the superior or knew the bishop of the diocese. Also, some sisters who recognized a need acted independently of any religious community and set out alone to respond to those needs wherever they surfaced." Many of the details of this account of the early days of St. Joseph's Hospital are taken from Sr. Mary Ellen Sprouffske's excellent research in "St. Joseph Regional Medical Center Celebrates 100 Years."
3. St. Louis archives
4. Rausch
5. Ames, 10
6. Ames
7. Coyne, 357-8
8. St. Louis archives
9. May 20, 1906 letter, St. Louis archives
10. "Early Pasco Physicians"

11. "Early Pasco Physicians"
12. "Early Pasco Physicians"
13. Ames, 31
14. Ames, 21
15. Ames, 23
16. St. Louis archives
17. St. Louis archives
18. St. Louis archives
19. St. Louis archives

CHAPTER 6
1. The history of the college is indebted to the long handwritten accounts of Sister Dolorosa, graduate of the Academy of Our Lady of Peace and one of the founders of the college. Preserved in the Los Angeles archives, "Mount St. Mary's College" and "Memories" tell the story from firsthand observation and are full of colorful details and good humor. I have quoted freely from these accounts.
2. Coyne, 311
3. Coyne, 312
4. Buildings were going up in nearby UCLA which had been founded in 1919.
5. Coyne, n. page 313
6. McCargar
7. McNeil, 4
8. McNeil
9. McNeil, 5
10. McNeil, 8
11. These memories of the sisters' early days at the Mount were shared with the author in the early 1960s.
12. McNeil, 42
13. McNeil, 56-57
14. In those days, the neighbors sometimes tended to be somewhat naïve. One of Sister Dolorosa's hysterical neighbors said after a 1938 fire: "I moved here because I thought the Sisters always chose safe places to build."
15. McNeil, 65
16. Edwards, 7

CHAPTER 7
1. Dart
2. Archives
3. During the changes after Vatican II, many sisters changed their religious names. Current names are used in this book for purposes of clarity.

4. "Celebrate the Spirit"
5. Coyne, 309

CHAPTER 8
1. Sprouffske, "The Center"
2. "Keeping Alive the Story"
3. "The Center"
4. "The Center"
5. "The Center"
6. *Design*
7. *Design*, iii
8. *Design*, 9-10

CHAPTER 9
1. June 3, 1971 letter from Sr. Carolyn Marie Armstrong, chair, Secretariat for Spiritual Renewal
2. Letter from Sr. Mary Brigid, May 8, 1974
3. Phan
4. Sr. Kathleen Mary McCarthy interview
5. Sr. Mary Brigid Fitzpatrick interview
6. Sr. Maureen O'Connor interview
7. The 1970s saw a decrease of about 176 sisters from 855 in 1970 to 679 in 1980. After 1980, the community lost about 100 sisters every ten years.
8. Clark
9. Chandler
10. Jennings
11. Jennings
12. The 2010-2011 annual report states that 4969 children and families were served that year by Casa de los Niños.

CHAPTER 10
1. "Farmworkers' Ministry Revisited"
2. Sr. Constance Fitzgerald interview
3. Archives
4. May 10, 1974 letter from Sr. Mary Brigid to the sisters of the Los Angeles Province
5. Passage from Steve Emerine, reporter for *The Arizona Daily Star*, read at Clare and Judy's funeral
6. Emerine
7. Harrington

8. Sullivan
9. Harrington
10. Sr. Louise Bernstein interview
11. Sr. Louise
12. Flyer announcing the new name
13. Lacher

CHAPTER 11
1. Sr. Kathleen Mary McCarthy interview
2. Sr. Joanna, March 6, 2013 letter
3. Murphy
4. Fitzgerald

CHAPTER 12
1. Mitchell
2. Mitchell
3. Coyne, 309
4. Sevilla

AFTERWORD
1. Sr. Mary McKay interview

WORKS CITED

BOOKS

Ames, Sr. Aloysia. *With You I Shall Always Be. Memoirs of Sisters of St. Joseph in Idaho and Eastern Washington.* Clarkston, WA: Clarkston Herald Printing Company, 1980.

Clark, Sr. Mary Kathleen. *A Dream Come True: the Story of Casa de los Niños.* 2nd ed. Tucson, Arizona: Arizona Lithographers, 1990.

Corrigan, Sr. Monica. *Trek of the Seven Sisters.* Los Angeles archives.

Coyne, Sr. St. Claire. "The Los Angeles Province." Part 5 of Dougherty, Sr. Dolorita Marie. *Sisters of St. Joseph of Carondelet.* St. Louis: B. Herder Book Co., 1966.

Design for Renewal of the Sisters of St. Joseph. St. Louis: Sisters of St. Joseph of Carondelet, 1967.

McNeil, Mary Germaine. *History of Mount St. Mary's College, Los Angeles, California 1925-1975.* New York: Vantage Press, 1985.

Murphy, Sr. Mary. *Homeless No More: A History of Good Shepherd Center for Homeless Women and Women's Stories.* Los Angeles, California: Sisters of St. Joseph of Carondelet and Good Shepherd Center, 1998.

Savage, Sr. Mary Lucida, compiler. *THE CENTURY'S HARVEST GATHERED BY THE SISTERS OF ST. JOSEPH OF CARONDELET IN THE UNITED STATES.* 1836-1936. (no date)

———. *The Congregation of Saint Joseph of Carondelet. A Brief Account of its origin and its work in the United States (1650-1922).* St. Louis: B. Herder Book Co, 1927.

ARTICLES

Cammack, Sr. Alberta. "History of St. Joseph's Orphan Home." Sr. Magdalen Gaffney's account, compiled by Cammack. *Designs,* March 2002.

———. "Mission San Xavier del Bac Celebrates 200 Years." *Designs,* April 1997.

———. "Sister Monica Corrigan, 1843-1929." 1999. Los Angeles archives.

———. "Florence, Arizona, 1883-1889." *Designs,* April/May 1998.

Celebrate the Spirit, 1954-1989: 35 years of excellence with compassion. Brochure celebrating the 35th anniversary of Daniel Freeman Hospitals, 1989.

Chandler, Russell. "Tucson 'Crisis Nursery' Pioneers in Effort to Prevent Child Abuse." *Los Angeles Times,* December 27, 1976.

Dart, John. "Biographer Details a Cardinal's 'Regime'." *Los Angeles Times,* June 7, 1997.

"Early Pasco physicians did operating in the kitchen." *Tri-City Herald*, February 27, 1949.

Edwards, Sr. Joseph Adele. "Women of Wisdom, Sowers of Seeds 1925-2000." *Facets of the Jewel*. Mount St. Mary's College publication in commemoration of the diamond anniversary of the college.

"Farmworkers' Ministry revisited." *Designs,* June 1998.

Fields, Sr. Mary Jean. *Reminiscences of the Sisters of St. Joseph of Carondelet and the Academy of Our Lady of Peace, 1882-1982.* (Originally appeared in the Summer 1982 issue of *The Journal of San Diego History.*)

Fitzgerald, Sr. Constance. "Read This if You Ever Doubted God's Determination." *Designs,* Dec. 2002.

Fleck, Ann Dietz, Sr. Mary Murphy, Sr. Mary Williams. *St. Mary's Academy: A Century of Excellence (1889).* 1989.

Harrington, Sr. Rose Cecilia. "Political Ministry." *Designs,* Nov. 1999.

Jennings, John. "Easing the Pain." *The Citizen,* May 11, 1996.

"Keeping Alive the Story." *Designs,* October 1995.

Lacher, Irene. "Serving the Homeless with a Touch of Class." *Los Angeles Times,* Sept. 13, 1999

Mannix, Sr. Mary Dolorosa. "Mount St. Mary's College." Manuscript, Los Angeles archives.

———. "Memories." Manuscript, Los Angeles archives.

McCargar, Victoria. "From the archives." *The Mount,* Summer/Fall 2011.

McNeil, Teresa Baksh. *St. Anthony's Indian School in San Diego, 1886-1907. The Journal of San Diego History.* Summer 1988, vol.34, no. 3.

Mitchell, Sr. Eileen. "The Associate Movement in the Los Angeles Province." Manuscript, Los Angeles archives.

"Moving into the 101st Year of the Deaf Ministry in the West." *Designs,* January 1996.

Phan, Sr. Eugenia. "With tears in our eyes." *Designs,* Nov. 1985.

Quinn, Sr. Mary Dorothea. "Early San Diego." *Designs,* July 2000.

Rausch, Sr. Mary St. John the Evangelist. Manuscript received from Sr. Dolorosa, Sisters of St. Joseph of Tipton, October 1975.

Schneiders, Sandra M., IHM. "That was Then….This is Now: The Past, Present, and Future of Women Religious in the United States." Women and Spirit Lecture, Saint Mary's College and University of Notre Dame, South Bend, Indiana, September 24, 2011.

Sevilla, Sr. Mary. "Circle the City." *Designs*, May 2008

Sprouffske, Sr. Mary Ellen. "The Center of the Western Province. Part III: West Los Angeles, California." *Designs*, March-April 1998.

———. "St. Joseph Institute, Oakland, CA." October 29, 1995. Los Angeles archives.

———. "St. Joseph Regional Medical Center Celebrates 100 Years." *Designs*, May-June 2002.

———. "Western Province established 120 years ago." *Designs*, April 1996.

Sullivan, Sr. Barbara. Unpublished essay on Sisters Clare Dunn and Judith Lovchik, Los Angeles archives.

OTHER

Benton, Sr. St. Charles, and Fields, Sr. Mary Jean. *Seventy-five Years in San Diego: Reminiscences of the Sisters of St. Joseph of Carondelet.* Unpublished manuscript, 1957. Los Angeles archives.

Corrigan, Sr. Monica. *Arizona—Missioners who went in 1873.* Notes, 1890. Los Angeles archives.

Diary of Sister Mary John Berchmans Hartrich, April 17, 1876 to June 18, 1876. Los Angeles archives.

McMahon, Sr. Thomas Marie. *The Sisters of St. Joseph of Carondelet: Arizona's Pioneer Religious Congregation, 1870-1890.* Master of Arts thesis, Graduate School of St. Louis University, 1952.

Smith, Sr. Ann Cecilia. "Education of the Deaf in California." In *Educational Activities of the Sisters of Saint Joseph of Carondelet in the Western Province—1870 to 1903.* Master of Arts thesis, The Catholic University of America, 1954.

Sprouffske, Mary Ellen. *Called Forth by the Dear Neighbor: Chronology of the Sisters of St. Joseph. 1648-2000.* Focus: Los Angeles Province of the Sisters of St. Joseph of Carondelet. Los Angeles archives.

About the Author

Sr. Mary Williams has been a Sister of St. Joseph of Carondelet for almost 60 years. Born and raised in Pasco, Washington, she is a graduate of The College of St. Catherine (now St. Catherine University) in St. Paul, Minnesota. After a year of study in Poitiers, France as a Fulbright scholar, she entered the Sisters of St. Joseph in Los Angeles and began a teaching career, having received her M.A. and Ph.D. in English and American Literature from Stanford University.

Sr. Mary has served as professor of English, academic dean, and provost at Mount St. Mary's College, Los Angeles. She has been active in leadership positions in the Los Angeles Province—as provincial councilor and regional superior, delegate to provincial chapters, and member of many committees, school and hospital boards, and activities over the years.

Retired as professor emeritus from the college, she lives currently in Pasco, Washington, continuing participation in province committees with a special interest in Mount St. Mary's College and CSJ-sponsored Lourdes Health Network, pursuing her favorite pastime of writing, and maintaining a book club with alumnae friends from the Mount.